A Migrant Heart

A Migrant Heart
DENIS SAMPSON

Copyright © 2014 Denis Sampson

This is a first edition.

All rights reserved. No part of this book may be reproduced, for any reason or by any means without permission in writing from the publisher.

Cover design: Debbie Geltner
Cover image: Eugene Beckes
Book design: WildElement.ca

Library and Archives Canada Cataloguing in Publication

Sampson, Denis, author   A migrant heart / Denis Sampson.

Issued in print and electronic formats.

ISBN 978-1-927535-47-9 (pbk.).--ISBN 978-1-927535-48-6 (html).--
ISBN 978-1-927535-49-3 (html).--ISBN 978-1-927535-50-9 (pdf)

1. Sampson, Denis. 2. Irish--Québec (Province)--Montréal--
Biography. 3. Irish Canadians--Québec (Province)--Montréal--
Biography. 4. Immigrants--Québec (Province)--Montréal--Biography.
5. Montréal (Québec)--Biography. I. Title.

FC2947.25.S24A3 2014   971.4'2800491620092   C2014-9026056
  C2014-902606-4

Printed and bound in Canada by Imprimerie Gauvin.

The publisher gratefully acknowledges the support of the Emerging Publisher Program of the Canada Council for the Arts

 Canada Council Conseil des arts
for the Arts   du Canada

Linda Leith Publishing Inc.
P.O. Box 322, Station Victoria, Westmount QC H3Z 2V8 Canada
leith.lindaleith@gmail.com
www.lindaleith.com

For Gay, searching in her own way,
whose love has been the greatest gift.

"…and I settle a migrant heart again in this otherwhere"

Eamon Grennan
"Dublin-Poughkeepsie: Bread Knife in Exile"

PROLOGUE

I am sitting in the Caffè Stella Polare in Trieste in the late afternoon. The brochure for the James Joyce walking tour led me to this café, where the Irishman had once spent evenings drinking. For the past hour or two I have been looking for some of the places associated with his decade of uncertain settling in Trieste a century ago, the years when he distanced himself from his childhood and youth in Dublin, and from the persona of the artist as superior young man. Here Joyce embraced Leopold Bloom, the down-on-his-luck, middle-aged Jew, as the hero of *Ulysses*, his book of wandering, and I try to imagine the crossroads of many cultures he found in this great commercial port of the Austro-Hungarian empire. Lovers and families now stroll on the *molos*, the broad quays that jut into the Adriatic, but there are no longer any ships setting out to travel the oceans, no sailors spending months at sea, finding their way by the Pole star.

I did not come here to follow the traces of my countryman's exile. Over the decades of my friendship with Iztok in Montreal, he has mentioned this city so often, and this region stretching from Venice to Ljubljana. It is the world of his first years before emigrating to Canada, of the past decade of regular returns, and of all his life, a place of shifting borders and histories, of nostalgia and brutality, of loss and desire. In print and over glasses of Tokaj, he has challenged the romantic images of Jan Morris, who writes about the city as "nowhere," and corrected Hemingway's superficial knowledge of the Italian-Slovenian borderlands and battlefields. Iztok has brought back wines for me from vineyards above Trieste, which all have their histories. We have actually met in Venice on the Zattere, and ate and drank in his haunts in Dorsoduro and Giudecca, but I have always known that this place farther east is Iztok's world, a place of nightmares and memories I could never hope to enter. Our friendship is of Montreal, the place of our displacement, and although he has not expressed any wish to visit Ireland, I have wanted for years to see his other place beyond Venice, beyond tourism, where corrections are always necessary.

I am sitting in the Caffè Stella Polare when I suddenly realize something about Iztok, and about myself. I realize that through all our years in Montreal, a Pole star has hovered above each of us. Whatever his friends might think of his obsessive and loving preoccupation with minute details of linguistic or historical accuracy, each detail is the trace of Slovenian lives that disappeared during the Italian occupation, or the German occupation that followed, or the Communist exterminations and silencings that came after. In the preface to a volume of his translations of the poems of Edvard Kocbek, he wrote: "In a country as small as Slovenia, what to you is history, is autobiography to me. The volume, like the lives of my parents, of Kocbek's generation, is divided into three parts: Before, During, and After. The During is the Second World War, a civil war in Slovenia, because of which I'm a Canadian and because of which my parents even now sigh, 'If things changed down there, we'd go back in a minute.'" But there is something about this sigh that reveals what he knows – that they would not go back. Nor did they, even when it became possible in the nineties, and in this they are like many post-war migrants in Canada. Following their "After," there was another After.

And as soon as I think of the celestial metaphor for Iztok's life, I remember standing with my father on a dark night some distance away from the farmhouse of my childhood in the west of Ireland and looking up at the night sky. More than fifty years ago, he showed me the stars that make up the Plough and how to find the North Star by following a line from the two stars at its extremity. This life-long farmer, my father, had ploughed these fields. He had no reason to know more than this one celestial formation, or indeed anything about the night sky except for signs he might find there that would help him predict the weather for the next day's work. He lived in the same place all his life, the farm on the shores of Lough Derg, on the border between counties Clare and Galway, and now I realize that this memory coming to me in the café in Trieste is offering me something for myself at this late stage of my life away from that countryside.

I

ONE

I am lying in the pram beside the breakfast room window, waking up from my afternoon nap. My mother must have positioned the pram here so that she could keep an eye on me from outside, where she is working in her flower garden. Suddenly, I am aware of her on the other side of the window looking in, waving to me and speaking. Something about her suggests urgency, anxiety, and it may be that I have drawn her attention by an effort to get out of the pram, or by rocking it, or perhaps I have cried out. We are separated by the glass of the high window, and it seems as if that prevents me from hearing her.

I know now it is possible to be heard through that window, but in my memory of the scene I believe she is calling to me and that her voice is lost. I expect she was urging me to stay still while she made her way up the path that ran alongside the house and around and in by the front door. I can remember no more than the expression on my mother's face, and maybe not even that, for the larger, compound memory that really remains is of my mother in her garden after she washed up the dinner things in the middle of the day and the men went back to work in the fields.

This first image of our separate worlds is of a time so early in my life that I doubt sometimes I do truly remember it. Perhaps it is one of those events remembered by her and retold to me so that I came to believe it is my own pure memory.

Yet that is unlikely for there is nothing for her to recall, unless I actually leaped from the pram. This was simply a fleeting image of mine, some tremor that touched a nerve inside me, perhaps her tension transplanted into me.

My mother's lost voice is less like a memory than an image from a mysterious or troubling dream, more like a prophecy of my own separation or silencing. Or perhaps the tension transplanted into me is the imprint of her sense of separation and silence, the record of her own exiled life in this surrogate home she had married into, and her desperate attachment to me.

It would take years for me to recognize such inner wells of feeling and begin to examine the tensions that drove her and were transplanted into my own life. The person I thought I knew was always active, a farmer's daughter from ten miles away, a farmer's wife, and she prided herself on her ability to get things done. She moved quickly and decisively, whether it was making her daily loaves of brown bread and white, and, once a week, fruitcake, queen cakes, or spotted dog; washing the clothes on Monday morning, hanging them out to dry on the line or stretched on the box hedges near the orchard gate, and then watching for signs of rain, and multiple trips in and out to test them, until she could get them dry enough for ironing; and then there were the animals – feeding hens and calves, washing the utensils in the dairy after the milking was done, morning and evening. The jobs were constant each day, each week, each year. "No rest for the wicked," she would say, repeating her mother's expression, although I don't think she believed she was in any way wicked. She was a silent worker who took no time to indulge in any sense of estrangement she might feel from where she was.

I came to know her garden well through all the summer days of my childhood: the fuchsia against the wall of the shed at the end, the overwhelming smell of lavender when I brushed against the big plants that overhung the narrow path, the multicoloured dahlias, the sweet william, the phlox, the carnations, the border plants, all mixed up in my mind but pleasing as I walked down the whole length of the garden for it was a surprise to come upon another dahlia or sweet william of a different colour from the last one.

My mother had a plan for the garden, even though it wasn't obvious to me. And she always seemed to have work to do in it, spring, summer, and autumn, moving a plant here or there, tidying up those that were dying off, watering, staking the tall ones, pruning and clipping: she never stopped. I knew that is how she wanted it to be, so that the time, her own time, was filled with love until she had to prepare the afternoon tea and the men had to be attended to once more.

Soon I recognized that her garden was different, essentially different from everything else in her life, the fierce energy and purpose that animated her around the house and in the farmyard different from the tension that went into the care of her pride and joy. In her garden she was a supreme artist. There she was far away from the place of her everyday limitations. And now I know that I too was her pride and joy, and that in some way, the creating of her garden and the dream she had for my life are connected.

*

There was no need to speak as we lifted the prow of the boat enough to ease it down the gravel so that it began to float on the shallow lake water. Only the bald coots in the reeds reacted, with a shriek and a flutter, the sounds echoing across the still bay. I got in first, my father's grip at the prow holding it firm while I stepped over seats and then sat at the back, my weight lifting the prow a little more off the gravel so that the entire boat was floating. Now he could leap on board and launch the boat all at once. A moment of uncertainty as he steadied himself, and then relief: the first part was done.

He stood by the middle seat and, taking one oar in silence, braced the tip in turn against the post of the boatshed, against the bluebell covered rock within jumping distance of the shore, against the stone embedded on the sandy bottom, moving the boat through a semi-circular reverse until finally the prow was pointing out into the bay and he could settle down with the two oars fitted over the tugpins; and then the even pull to the fishing place could begin.

I always hung over the back watching the perch fry scatter from the sandy shallows as the boat turned, and then, as we moved into open water, watched out for the tall rushes ahead, much taller than me if I stood up, for if the boat cut through a grove of rushes I would quickly grab one as they passed and try to cut the tough green tube against the edge of the boat. You had to be fast, all one motion, or you lost the chance as the boat sped by, and it often happened that the rush was too tough for my little hands and wouldn't cut through in time, and as I looked back in regret I would see the tall graceful stem bent over, damaged, and I would catch a glimpse then of the stone farmhouse on the hillside above the lake as it receded into the distance.

We reached the mouth of the bay near the island, and it was time to let out the lines. My father stopped rowing and put away the oars. We had the lake to ourselves these Sunday mornings after Mass. There was no one trolling in our bay and, as far as we could see, there were no boats between ourselves and the Tipperary hills a few miles across the water. Sometimes it was cloudy or rainy, the slate-blue surface mirroring the sky, but my father thought this the best weather for fishing. Best too was a gentle breeze that scarcely rippled the water but was enough to carry the drifting boat once the baited lines were let out. The two slender rods were the length of the boat, like wands anchored against the tugpins, one on either side.

We drifted in a trance of stillness and anticipation. My father took out a cigarette and lit up. He smoked Sweet Afton, and it was on one of these mornings that he read out to me the words of Robert Burns on the gold and white box. "Flow gently, sweet Afton, among thy green braes / Flow gently, I'll sing thee a song in thy praise." They were the only lines of poetry he ever read to me, ever read for himself, it may be, for he was not a reader. He was a farmer who never in his whole lifetime read a book or often took much interest in the printed word.

The only part of the *Irish Independent* he took seriously was the page of death notices. The entire back page was full of these notices, and I remember he turned first to that page. The test of its value to him was, of course, that he might find there the announcement of someone's death, someone he knew from the village or neighbouring villages, whose funeral he should attend. If he found such an announcement, he would read it out to my mother; that was the only thing he ever read out to her, the only news that really seemed to have a bearing on his life, apart from the cattle market report and the weather forecast which preceded the evening news on Radio Eireann.

So this moment when he read the fragment of Burns is memorable, the only suggestion I can recall that my father could appreciate lyrical language or any literary effect whatsoever. The smell of the bluish smoke and the cool of the lakewater and the empty sky mingled with the lyrics of Burns and with my father as he was in that interlude. Ever after, whenever he took out his cigarettes, I thought of the words of Burns that had transformed the lake that I knew, and ever after, this Shannon lake was every other magical lake, of Wordsworth and Yeats especially.

The setting out across the bay towards the island, the silence and the stillness, remain with me, more pleasurable than what came later. After his second or third cigarette, after drifting across the bay once or twice, sometimes we'd hear a tremor on the line as the hook snagged a weed, then our first real bite, and my father would jump into action, grabbing the rod as the line began to run out from the screaming reel, and the tip of the rod curved with the strain as he slowly began to wind it in and let it go again, playing the fish as his excitement built, suddenly finding words, speculating about the size, hoping his catch would stay hooked, waiting for the moment when he would sense the fish growing tired, fighting with less strength against the relentless winding in, until suddenly the fish would break the surface of the water, and my father would spot him parting the water as he came towards us, struggling.

"Pass me the net," my father would direct me, and with one hand he would jerk the fish out of the water with a sweep of the rod while with the other he would stretch out the net and capture it. The tension would subside at that instant, for sometimes at the final stage, as the fish came towards the boat, or even in the netting action, the fish would wriggle off the hook. But now it was in, the hook removed from its bleeding gills, and it was on the floorboards flapping its tail in terror, so that its whole body flipped over and back in my direction. This was the part I didn't like, and it could go on for a long time, the flapping and jerking becoming intermittent, the fish slowly dying on the boards.

By now my father had quickly reset the line and probably had another perch landed or had grown immune to the presence of the first one, resuming his patient watch in silence, his bluish smoke drifting skywards. At the end of the morning, when we would hear my mother blowing the whistle to call us in to dinner, we might have three, four, or five perch, and after we returned to the boathouse and tied the boat to the post, he would take out his penknife, cut a hazel sapling, a good one that had a fork, and on it he would suspend the fish by driving it though their bleeding gills.

It is the sound of the flapping fish that I still remember, the slow dying, and even though my father liked the companionship, and I went with him for years, I did not become a fisherman. After I began to read, I would bring along a book and, to his disgust, spend my time lost in it, sitting at the back of the boat.

★

I knew the stillness and the quiet on the lake suited him, reflected his own nature. I accepted his solitary behaviour in this patient, contemplative role as his way of being, and accepted it for myself too. Although I did not become a fisherman, the lake was central to his life and in some way, I now imagine, its disciplines of silence became central to mine too.

On Sunday mornings, and every evening in summertime, he went trolling for trout or perch; in May, it was the dapping, floating the May-fly on the surface, or dry-fly fishing, and in season, he set lines for eels that he would check at dawn. In shooting season, he had various hiding places in the rushes along the shoreline where he would wait for wild duck. The practical benefits of his fishing and shooting activities, and the pleasure he derived from bringing in a good catch, were secondary, I believe, to the experience of being there, close to the water, and I often wonder about the intimacy between the lake and my father's inner life that had grown over a lifetime. He was not a nature mystic, nor indeed did he pay particular attention to any aspects of nature that were not of immediate use to him; nor was he a religious man, yet the routines of his relationship with the lake had established a bond that was consoling, calming, restorative of an inner peace, an anchor that is often associated, in the simplest and most profound ways, with prayer and religious ceremonies.

Apart from being an extension of the house and the farm, it sometimes seemed that the social life of the house yielded place to the reality of the lake and the river Shannon it was part of. It was a separate water world that we could see from the house, its character changing from minute to minute. As the wind rose or fell, it could be placid or wave-tossed, a translucent mirror or a dark place of upheaval and whitecaps, a place for languorous sailing on the far shore at Dromineer or a treacherous waterway that would empty of all boats when storms blew up.

As the light was filtered by the clouds passing above, or by all the variations of mist and rain, it could be a surface so clean and clear that the Tipperary hills seemed only yards away or an impenetrable space of darkness and foreboding. Long before I had read Wordsworth's poems of his lakeland in all its moods, my lake had become part of me, as I think it was part of my father. Reading its character, respecting its separate reality, were habits of mind for both of us.

But if I felt that my father was in his true element here, by this lake where he had spent his entire life, the house and farm too were part of who he was. On the lake, he seemed to have a kind of respect for its authority and its mystery, his silence here a kind of awe that I also knew from going to Mass. But his taciturn character became a deeper and more troubling mystery.

It was not only on the lake that he was silent but in the house also, with my mother, and around the farmyard, going about his business; and in the village, too, he was clearly not one of those who drew pleasure from conversation. He had to join the men who lined up by the wall outside the chapel after Sunday Mass, for the women had their own conversations, but there was little enthusiasm in his participation. In so many small ways, being in his presence in the early years, conscious of his great unease and tension when he met other people, I knew that to him conversation equalled a risky social engagement.

He was fearful of other people, perhaps only of their verbal skills, their wit, their jokes and stories, their confident social presence, their pleasure in interaction; but being ill at ease, being shy or tongue-tied, was hardly the whole explanation. Certainly he was shy, and had little ability in spontaneously reaching out to the other person. He was a loner, too, for there were very few people he spent any time with, not even his younger brother or neighbours. I knew that he once used to go to the pub for a pint now and then and had been a keen card-player – he told with pleasure of all-night sessions and weekend card-parties in his youth – but all this had ended, apparently, when he married my mother. There were one or two people he trusted and would go fishing or shooting with, as he had done since childhood, but I could tell that his heart wasn't really in these companionable activities.

After I recognized this, the mystery for me was why this might have happened, if indeed there was any particular turning point that had resulted in his suspicion of others. Had he been betrayed? Was his shyness due to some earlier sense of incompetence or shame? Was he simply a quiet countryman who had settled into his late marriage, and in middle age had left aside more youthful social impulses? Was his silence a consequence of his marriage to my mother, or was this a fundamental orientation of his personality? And of mine?

The house had a past, a history of bitter family conflicts in earlier generations and again in my father's own lifetime, for the property had been awkwardly divided between him and his brother. He sometimes told of how he had been the victim of the transaction, duped by his bossy sister and her solicitor, that he had been given the lesser portion, the poorer land, fields without stock, a house without furniture, and so on, and how he had recovered from this unjust disadvantage by his own efforts, and certainly not because of any assistance given by his sister and brother. My father no longer talked to him, and this disagreement had, in my mind, a deeper significance than the unfair division of property. My uncle was a talker, a gregarious, hard-drinking individual, known far and wide through his interests in sports, especially greyhound racing and horse racing, but these activities were merely the counters in a life of pleasure-seeking and camaraderie. Son of a landowner, he was somewhat déclassé in his habits and pursuits, for the pub is a great leveller in Irish society, and the contrast between the brothers was something my mother was keenly aware of. She seemed to believe that, from an early age, the spoiled younger brother had overshadowed in so many ways my father's development and fortune.

The long isolation of that house in its own world by the lakeside, in its many layers of withdrawal and inwardness, gave me a sense of something beautiful and a training in contemplation. It also gave me something else: a detachment, a turning away towards reading and the contemplation of natural beauty, and also a suspicion of people's motivations and the forces that guide human history.

*

On Sunday afternoons while my father dozed in the armchair, listening to Micháel Ó Heither's commentary on the hurling match, my mother took my brother and me to visit Dolly and the Major. They lived a short distance down the road in a rented house overlooking the harbour. Major Gibson was probably approaching eighty years of age, and Dolly was his maid, companion, and nurse.

Like my mother, Dolly was a very keen gardener, and this was the reason for our visits. After tea and biscuits and some lame conversation in the sitting room – during which the Major poured himself whiskey and used his mysterious silver soda siphon with great ceremony – they would spend the remainder of the afternoon viewing the extensive flowerbeds. Bored, my brother and I would explore the watery jungle beyond the harbour. My mother would usually return home with some cuttings or roots.

Dolly and the Major had blown in a few years earlier. Neither of them had any children or family connections in that part of the country, and his stories were drawn from a lifetime spent in various British colonies all over the globe: India, Malaysia, Kenya. On Sundays, he attended the service in the Church of Ireland in Mountshannon, but it was remarked that he always drove Dolly to Mass and was always on time. In his final years, this old man had found a place to attach himself to.

In the nineteenth century, Williamstown Harbour and Hollands' Pier, a few hundred yards farther on, were stopping places for commercial and passenger boats on the Shannon. In the grounds there had once been a hotel with a large courtyard. One could easily imagine it as a resort hotel with a view across Lough Derg to County Tipperary, but in my childhood it was an empty shell, a ruin slowly being enveloped by giant cedars and a jungle of rhododendrons, laburnum, apple trees and shrubs already untended for decades.

The end of its first life came with the arrival of Bianconi cars and railways. It was no longer a place of importance for river traffic, and the hotel eventually became a summer residence for a succession of English families. But a more spectacular end came in 1920 when four young men, on the run, were discovered hiding there. They were from nearby villages and towns, most likely involved in ambushes of British soldiers by the East Clare Brigade. The young men were taken by the Black and Tans, brought by truck to the bridge in Killaloe, and executed on the parapet. In retaliation, the IRA burned it to the ground.

In later decades, the harbour and grounds were bought by Dublin people as a holiday place. Next to the abandoned ruin, they built a wooden bungalow with a veranda along the front, a strange architectural exhibit in this countryside of thatched cottages and stone farmhouses. While the structure itself suggested warmer climates – India perhaps – its creosoted exterior and the unlighted interior gave it a dominant feeling of gloom and suffocation.

During the time we used to call on Dolly and the Major, the "black bungalow" was also rented, by a mysterious man who did not socialize with them and would have nothing to do with anyone in the neighbourhood. He was not a gardener or a fisherman, and, indeed, it was not so clear what kind of haven the harbour offered to him. In fact, my father knew him by reputation; he was one of three brothers who had been leaders of the East Clare Brigade. Thirty years before, they had been legendary, but I discovered that after the Treaty and the establishment of the Irish Free State, this man had left the country, and found a job in the British Post Office, in the capital city of his former enemy. More puzzling still is that he should have come to spend his retirement years in Williamstown, for it is almost certain that the brothers had a hand in the burning of the mansion, in the grounds of which he had now become a recluse.

One day near the harbour, my brother and I were stopped by a man who spoke in an American accent, although he threw in teasing expressions in Irish, "you guys" mixing with *buachaills*. We guessed that he was The Yank who had recently bought the Williamstown property, a local man who had spent most of his adult life in the United States. In time, we learned that he had worked as a car mechanic in forty-nine different states, and during his years as a restless migrant, he had developed all kinds of practical skills and a philosophy of self-help to go with them. He had already started work on the renovation of the mansion as a business venture, a hotel, or apartments, he explained, and he planned to do most of it with his bare hands.

Over the next years, he often invited us down to admire his progress. He planned to restore the front portion first, but after a year of work, he abandoned this project. Beginning again, he focused on the back portion; he brought this section of three town houses close to completion, but abandoned it too. Next he set about building a house for himself on a small piece of land separated from the places of his earlier labours by a site he had sold. In our minds, it was a kind of treehouse, built against a steep hill, without back windows or doors, wedged between two old trees.

By then, the rented houses were vacant, the blow-ins departed, and I had reached the age for departure too. But Williamstown stays in my mind as a haven that had drawn these unattached and wandering men in their later years and offered some calm for whatever restlessness had driven them in their earlier decades. It strikes me too that the quiet place in which I spent those first years disclosed many small reminders that the world stretched far away into other countries and continents and that a single lifetime could include many phases and transformations.

TWO

Every Christmas we drove to Limerick, thirty miles away, for a shopping spree. My mother and father would often have serious business to do — a watch to be repaired at Hartman's, a machine part to be bought at Speight's — but the trip always included a visit to Santa Claus at Todd's on O'Connell Street. We would have lunch in the dining room of the Savoy, the wide staircase and the lobbies leading to the cinemas all carpeted, so that in my mind it was the height of luxury. We never went to the cinema, not for all the years of my childhood, but the film posters were part of the exotic urban experience that the Savoy represented.

It was my mother's brother Frank who bought *Robinson Crusoe* as a Christmas present when I was five and my brother seven, and without her prompting, he would never have thought of such a thing. He did not read books, any more than my father did. On this occasion, I can see us going into the APCK, just up the street from Todd's, and turning right down the stairs into the children's department. I have the book still, a very fat volume with large print and a cream dustjacket with an illustration of Crusoe on his island, holding a shepherd's staff and dressed in animal skins, a large, tropical bird sitting on his shoulder. It was a cheap edition, abridged for children, in the days before attractive paperbacks made books more seductive, but the cover hardly mattered to me, so great was my tension and theirs in the buying of this book. This was a big event in all our lives.

It seems to me now that it was my first experience of entering a bookshop, but this may only be due to the tension of this occasion. Why the book was bought in the APCK shop I don't know, rather than in O'Mahony's across the street. I knew there was something strange about this shop, and after I learned to read, I was able to decipher the words that went with the acronym, the Association for the Promotion of Christian Knowledge, and, sure enough, there were many bibles and prayer books prominently displayed here, while in its mirror image across the street, there were missals and Catholic Truth Society pamphlets, rosary beads too, and statues of the Blessed Virgin, the Sacred Heart and favourite saints.

What remains a puzzle is why *Robinson Crusoe* was bought in a Protestant bookshop, for then and on my own later visits to the children's department, there was an aura of transgression, of risk, perhaps even of fear, for it seemed that already I was travelling through unknown and dangerous territories, almost like going into a Protestant church.

The simple truth was probably that it was not available in O'Mahony's, and my mother was determined to have it. It was my first book, this the first occasion when I experienced the ritual of searching and finding a book, buying, and then the pleasure of anticipation, until the title page was turned and Chapter One lay waiting. My mother read it for us, one chapter at a time, gathered around the fire in the drawing room where we sat on winter nights. This was the moment when my mother translated her desire for another life for me into a concrete step. She was determined that reading would occupy a central place in my life, and already I knew from her that reading and going away were in some way connected. My brother would inherit the farm, and I would be sent away to boarding school, and after that to the city, and, as it turned out, I would keep going and end up living in another country.

And so it was that when I rowed out to the island in the Shannon or to isolated points on the wooded shore, I became Crusoe. My boyish fantasies while building treehouses or hacking my way through the dense jungle of briars and bushes, were coloured with solitariness, and my dread of encountering cannibals on the lakeshore went deeper than childish fears and nightmares. It was the fragility of my own identity in that place which was threatened with extinction.

In my solitary adventures, transported to islands far from there, the romance of shipwreck and survival was the underlying myth, and in that charged and scary story, I was conspiring with those forces of estrangement which would shape me. If I was fated to become Crusoe, and so abandoned, maybe I could also become the heroic Crusoe, master of himself and of his island.

*

From my first day in the village school, I had a new name. In the Department of Education roll book, my Anglo-Norman family name was given an Irish version, invented on the spot by the principal teacher. My first name, French Catholic after St. Denis, first bishop of Paris, was also changed, and so I became Donnacha Ó Samsúin. Each day for years, it was called out, and I would answer *Anseo*, meaning "Here! I'm here!" This renaming was my first real experience of translation, of dislocation, for even as I insisted I was here, the very grounds of my attachment to home were being put in doubt. The state of being here and securely in my own self was constantly questioned, as it were, by a contrary version of here and selfhood, which had the imprimatur of the official authorities and their interpretation of history.

A child grows, of course, inside layers of expectations that come to him from many sources, and his own desires and talents are shaped within and against those expectations. My father spoke no Irish, and although my mother had learned it in school, she had no interest in speaking it; in fact, I never heard either of them utter a word of Irish. But in school, so much of the teaching was done in Irish that we took it for granted that our "native language" was something we had to master to become an authentic Irishman – not simply to qualify to work in the civil service, as we learned very early on, but in some vague psychological and moral sense. It was clear that a kind of superiority was available to those who spoke the language, and the fact that I was disinherited of my original name was simply a necessary price. It was merely a kind of bookkeeping, a part of how my education would shape me and make me a better person than my parents were.

For years I had heard its strangeness on the radio. *An Nuacht* came on each evening after the children's programs and the Angelus. There would be news items about *an Oireachtas* and *an Taoiseach*, the newsreader swirling those vowels until they were gulped down with the consonants. You had to do something special with your mouth to produce such sounds, but I learned that these were native speakers, Irish was their first language, and so they spoke with an authentic intonation, usually called the *blas*. Strange as it sounded, we would have to make this way of speaking our own; we would have to get used to hearing ourselves in another voice. It was not good enough to know the other language, to read it or write it in school, for it was oral Irish that really counted: we would have to retune our tongues to produce a better voice than the one that we had naturally grown into in our homes.

This was the official project of cultural renewal already established in the schools since the thirties, but somehow in that small school, I can now see, there was room for the complications and nuances of belief and dissent, of robust selfhood and undermining doubt, of multiple levels of communication, which, after all, is how life presents itself to us once we grow beyond school and the first official simplicities. And the expectations of adults can be communicated in many different ways, many of them implicit and probably even unconscious. The school principal, a local man whose intellectual ability had allowed him to transcend his background, used the Irish form of his name, Pádraig Ó hEaráin, and devoted a considerable amount of time to teaching Irish, but I now find it odd that my memories of him recover what I think most impressed me and made him a very distinct individual.

Before nature study or the environment were heard of in schools, he brought the landscape alive for me in ways farming people like my father never could. Because of his passion for walking, he revealed the countryside to us as a place of wonder and beauty. He would routinely direct our attention to the plants in season and encourage us to collect unusual specimens and share them with the class. I was converted to this kind of looking, to the appreciation of the distinctive things that were revealed through close examination, and so interested did I become that I won first prize for the best collection of wild flowers at the Scariff Agricultural Show.

Our principal was also a reader – in English. I can still see the County Librarian arriving each month in his van to replace the selection of books, about twenty of them, which were left on a bench near the door. I usually read them all before he returned – Biggles books, the Hardy Boys, and the Kestrels – and I recall the teacher encouraging this. I knew that he was a man with a passion for learning, and that he cared about language and self-expression, but all this was coloured in striking ways by his primary avocation: acting with the local drama group each winter.

In the weeks after Christmas, he gave us work to do while he learned his lines. We knew it was just to keep us quiet, and we cooperated, pretending to pore over our copybooks, memorizing a poem, writing a composition, or doing sums, while our real attention went to the actor with his back to us, staring out the window. I remember best *The Playboy of the Western World,* probably because I saw the play at the Drama Festival. In class, we watched as he muttered words we couldn't quite hear and tried out "faces" and tones of voice. He wasn't just reciting something the way we recited "The splendour falls on castle walls," or "He cannot hear the bittern cry / In the wild sky where he is lair." – words and phrases we rattled off as if they had no meaning. But we listened to him in fascination as he brought the words to life. "He's not my father. He's a raving maniac would scare the world." He was oblivious to us now, his voice becoming clearer. He had another audience in his head. Gradually he was easing into the spirit of the character so much that his voice would get loud enough for us to hear: "Shut your yelling, for if you're after making a mighty man of me this day by the power of a lie, you're setting me now to think if it's a poor thing to be lonesome, it's worse maybe to go mixing with the fools of earth."

His voice would raise and lilt and rant. We knew nothing about the play itself, but there in our classroom was another kind of play. He was becoming someone else. He was finding a way of saying the words so that he was no longer himself, but his animation seemed to say that the other self was more interesting or more real. We didn't know what was supposed to be happening in that other life, but, day after day, watching him slip away through those words was as good as being at the Drama Festival itself.

Our principal's performance in Synge's play was acclaimed. He won the best actor award, and the production went on to the All-Ireland finals in Athlone. I can't remember what happened next, for this much glory for my teacher was as much as I could imagine. But now, many years after his death, his performance lives on in me, and I have no doubt that his love of language and eloquence affected me greatly. I might have developed a love of language and literature anyway, but his transformation of himself and his role as teacher through the assumption of another voice was the major lesson he taught in that school. But it was a literary voice, in English, not the *blas* or the role of the native speaker. This was a different kind of self-transformation.

*

When I look back at that time, I realize that the official goal for young people of embracing the "national language" coincided with a different and more fundamental linguistic transformation that I was undergoing. I was becoming educated, and in the process was growing away from the world of my father. My mother had always encouraged reading, and as I became aware of written language as a kind of enriched norm of discourse in the greater world, I noticed the local features of my father's speech. He had grown up and lived all his life on the farm in a part of the country that had many Irish speakers until late in the nineteenth century. There were local expressions and pronunciations that owed much to that oral culture.

I was an impatient teenager. I was ashamed of my father's accent and his limited literacy. He did not read books or write anything except his signature on cheques. When I remember him, I hear a character whose speech might be branded as stage-Irish, a literary conceit in the representation of Irish peasants on the London stage or in novels during the nineteenth century. But in fact this was his speech and the speech of the country people around me as I grew up. There were no pigs or hens under our kitchen table, but as we sat around it, there were so many words and phrases that the Oxford English Dictionary would not find a place for: *scuther, geansai, ownseach*.

My father was most himself in the clichés and proverbs that were current in that parish between the mountains and the lake. I wrote down many of his expressions as a marker of my own separation from him and from the community. When I read them now, I see that they have a remarkable colour, entirely suited to his way of life: "She'd herd weasels at a crossroads," "he was as old as the hills," "it could happen to a bishop," "as deaf as a stone wall," and "'tis easily known he's from the mountain." But if my father were to be my role model in any sense, my first language, his language, would have to fit me, and the more I became educated, the less this was possible.

His speech was close to being a separate dialect of English, certainly not the voice I heard on the radio, the educated voice of Dubliners, or the levelled voice I was exposed to in my boarding school in Roscrea, for in that Cistercian college, there were boys from all over the country. Nor did it occur to me that the layering of expression in the countryside was an emblem of settlement, and of enrichment, a resource out of which great poetry could be written. Seamus Heaney's capacity for digging into the soil of his place, into the strata of the English language, and finding in language itself a metaphor for the expanding and inclusive range of his experience, was not available to me. Heaney's embrace of the home turf gave him a secure base onto which everything could be added with confidence. I understand fully his admiration for another farm boy, Patrick Kavanagh, for when I read *Tarry Flynn*, I thought this autobiographical novel described exactly the world I knew in childhood. In the case of Heaney's country speech, everything extra was a cause of celebration; he did not seem to undergo the anxiety of assimilation that eroded my confidence in my paternal tongue. My guilty sense of needing to be distant from my father and his place, my anxious uprootedness, began early so that I no longer had a home turf in either English or Irish.

More complicated still was the role of my mother, for it was she who wanted me educated and away from the farm. Whether she actually knew it or not, she didn't want me to be like him, and even though Irish was required for a civil service job that she wished me to have in Dublin, in her heart she believed that Irish was backward. English was not only her own language but was associated in her mind with success and "the right kind of people."

It was not that she would want me to deliberately change my accent, for she, like most country people, had a critical ear for local people who went away to England or America and came back with new accents. It was common to hear people remark, with mixed feelings of superiority and resentment, on the affected or pretentious accent of those emigrants who had consciously or unconsciously adopted the speech of their workmates or neighbours. By adopting airs and graces, they had sold out on their first bonds and loyalties and had turned their backs on those who had remained behind to live out their lives in their one and only voice.

My mother's encouragement of my efforts to look out and away led me to unconsciously adopt a somewhat more educated speech. From an early age, I had listened every evening to children's programs on Radio Eireann. On the radio I could hear all the variations of the regions, Cork and Kerry, the Northern counties, the Dublin suburbs, and all the recognizably local inflections, but I knew that they stood out from the standard educated speech that radio people used. If I came to have a generic Irish accent rather than a Clare accent, it came about through listening to the radio and going away to boarding school.

But now I know that the rejection of my father and of the home turf left hidden scar tissue. And what I heard on the radio wasn't all so easily assimilated. I wanted to be part of that world elsewhere, but there were some aspects of it with which I was uncomfortable. Why was it that educated people seemed to have an aura of English power about them, an aura of Empire? Why was it that the man who spoke about birds in the Irish countryside was named J. Ashton Freeman? With a name like that, he was hardly someone who had grown up in the countryside about which he talked so knowledgeably. The dramatized narratives from Irish history, episodes on the Flight of the Earls and the Battle of Clontarf, were prepared by G.A. Hayes-McCoy. A double-barrelled name always betokened Empire in my mind.

Although many Irish people have refined antennae for such matters as accent, name, and origin, it may be that I was unusually sensitive because I was not secure about my own name. It had come to Ireland with the Anglo-Normans in the twelfth century. The ancestral land outside Kilkenny (no doubt originally granted to followers of Strongbow, the leader of the first Norman settlers) caught the attention of Cromwell many centuries later, and so, being Catholics, the occupants and their retinue (perhaps among those of Norman origin who were said to have become "more Irish than the Irish themselves") were expelled, and wandered for a generation or two in Cork and Limerick before going to Clare in 1698, after the settlements following the Siege of Limerick. In the centuries after they were forced to choose, to move "to Hell or to Connaught," many of their descendants married locally, and so my mother's name was O'Grady, her mother's name Hynes; my paternal grandmother's name O'Brien.

The legal invisibility of those mothers of Gaelic paternity made a historical fantasy about the purity of the foreign name possible, but if a bloodline means anything, it is surely a matter of genetics not pedigree. And the farm I grew up on came into my family in the early nineteenth century when the heir, a Protestant woman named Brady, married my great-great grandfather. Out of the confusion of the conversions and pretend conversions and legal manoeuvres of the eighteenth century, surprisingly, this young woman had emerged a landowner with tenants around the edge of the farm. By the time my father was born, there were no longer tenants, but I grew up feeling that in the eyes of some I was an outsider, a usurper of something native, and the name I happened to bear was the emblem of that estrangement.

★

Just inside the front door of my house in Montreal is a painting my elder son made for me. It is one of many around the house, some of them figure studies from live models, and landscapes from his travels in Morocco and Ireland. This one he worked up from an old photograph taken by my wife on Lough Derg.

It looks back to a time more than thirty years ago. I am in the centre, a large figure sitting in a small boat, rowing. In front of me are two young boys wearing Montreal Expos baseball caps, himself and his young brother, one on either side of me, looking off in different directions. The prow of the boat is behind me, of course, so that the perspective lines lead to the open water of the lake. Over my left shoulder, in the distance, is a suggestion of an island, towards which the boat might be moving.

The sun is somewhere behind us, so that our faces are in shadow but, at any rate, I am sporting a large amount of hair and beard, still red at that time, and my sons' expressions are also indistinct because of the baseball caps pulled low over their eyes. That is how it was on that day, I like to think, that is how the camera captured it, and it was no lack of talent that left the faces indistinct, for it is our bodies in the boat and our relationships to each other inside the frame that is the essence of the picture.

My son may have had his own reasons for choosing the photograph: painterly ones – perhaps the composition of the figures, the play of light and shade, his wish to experiment with browns and blues – but, in his own way, he was probably drawn to the narrative of family life that exists there in an instantaneous fragment. Casual viewers might think it simply a sentimental record of a camping holiday in Vermont or Quebec, and the photograph, before it was painted, was little more than that, although who is to say that the sentimental gesture does not contain a more lasting joy? He remembers the sense of adventure out on the lake; he memorializes the depth of his own experience back then, in that place, as well as, I assume, his pleasure in my presence as oarsman.

But the depth of the paint, its sombre tones, the arrested and statuesque postures of the figures, the water, the boat, all mark this as an interpretation of another kind, an epic passage. After all, he chose this particular scene, and he painted it for me. He too was looking back to something he had known as a child. It is a tribute to our family bond, to our solidity as we moved off over and over into the unknown of the future and of our lives. We have, all three, grown in our different directions over the decades since the moment it records, but we are all timelessly together. He has used his talent to put us forever inside that frame, as intimately placed as we were in the boat.

Captured in seconds by my wife sitting at the stern, this was a photograph of me rowing my father's boat on the lake where I had grown up. This was the Shannon lake, which could be seen from all the fields of the farm and from the house surrounded by a medley of trees: chestnut, beech, ash, sycamore, birch, and firdale. In fact, as we sit in the boat, we are looking back towards the boathouse, the wooded shore, the fields sloping up to the house, and the house itself, from which I had often taken my bearings in boyhood as I rowed out the bay towards the island.

This is an image of family intimacy in which my son memorialized his own feeling of that morning on the lake, and of being at his paternal grandparents' house in summertime, and in the place of my childhood. But it radiates ironies for me. Apart from the imagery of the boat that is carrying us, of the setting out with our backs to the future, of the vague island that is the goal of my efforts, the fact is that I left this place of my childhood; I left my family behind, I separated myself not only from them but from the country and culture of my first years. I became a kind of exile, a traveller, an immigrant in the French-speaking city of Montreal, and it was here that I became a husband and father, and a new family formed, and it was from here that over the decades we returned to visit the place of my beginning.

I was brought up knowing that I would not make my life on the farm, that I would be going away to boarding school – the only way for a farm boy to have secondary education before busing was introduced in 1968 – and after that to the city. Lost in books, I played at being shipwrecked on that island, like Robinson Crusoe, or the boys on Coral Island. I played at learning how to be alone elsewhere. My brother, who knew he was going to inherit the farm, played with Meccano sets (and would become a skilled mechanic), absorbed the rudiments of animal husbandry (and would later own a pedigree herd), and was already trying his hand at driving my uncle's tractor. Without knowing it, I too was preparing, in my case for departure.

The Shannon lake could never be a holiday place for me. Nor was there great pleasure in returning until I went back with my children, and through them and their joyous attachment to this beautiful lakeside, I began to imagine the countryside of my childhood as I had once imagined an elsewhere. I wanted to give them the childhood experience I never truly had in this place, to simply be there at play in the fields and the woods and on the lake. I wanted them to see the beauty rather than the harshness, to experience the pleasure and the freedom rather than the repression and the guilt of being different, destined to leave, destined to betray the life I had been given in this place.

And perhaps my son's painting captures no more than this, his pleasure in being in an ancestral place, mine alone the burden of memory and reflection, of imagining the silent, conflicted histories that shaped so many of the lives of people rooted there and also of those who, like me, went elsewhere.

Sitting on my desk now is a photograph of me holding my son's daughter when we visited the farm together some years ago for my niece's wedding. The desk is at a high window of this old house in Montreal, and I am looking out from this great room in which I am surrounded by all the books I have accumulated since I first arrived here four decades ago, many of them mirrors that have allowed me to imagine for a time this life between here and there.

THREE

On Sunday afternoons, we sometimes went for drives away from the farm in our first car, a dark-green second-hand Morris Minor. The road we took passed by Drewsboro, the home of my father's cousins, the O'Briens. We always slowed down to catch sight of the tall redbrick house set on a slope a few hundred yards back from the main road. You couldn't see much of it because of the mature beeches, ash, and chestnut trees around the entrance gate and the avenue that led to the house. When we arrived at the house of my mother's cousin in O'Callaghan's Mills, I would hear my mother make comments about the state of Drewsboro now – the neglected fences, or the ragwort all over the lawn, or the poor quality of the unfertilized grass.

"Wouldn't you think they'd be mortified by the cut of the place? What's going to be the end of them at all?"

We never visited the O'Briens, even though Michael and my father were first cousins and had seen much of each other when they were young. All the O'Brien cousins lived for periods in my father's house – the house of my own childhood – where my grandmother took care of them. It was explained to me that Michael's father and mother "drank themselves to death," and that the same fate had befallen another pair of O'Brien parents, another uncle and aunt of my father.

I had been reading children's editions of Dickens, and so I thought I recognized a Victorian picture of predestined ends, with orphans passed around from house to house. The drunken mania and early death of all these O'Briens illustrated the melodramatic catastrophes that seemed to fit my own moral world. After all, we heard over and over, in church, in school, and at home, that "you know not the day nor the hour" of God's final intervention. A pious child, I lived from Confession to Confession in case my immortal soul would be stained when the Final Judgment came.

It is clear to me now that Michael himself in his adulthood had become a scandalous person. He too, it seemed, was well on his way to drinking himself to death. Much of his farm had been claimed piecemeal by the bank. The loss of fields, in a community of farmers who valued land more than their own children, was the ultimate disgrace, and so I imagined Drewsboro as a decaying mansion enveloped as in a Gothic novel by ancestral fears and curses.

And while my own childish imagination was transforming this place into vague images from fiction that corresponded with the needs of my moral world, my cousin, Edna, the daughter of this house, was also at work, in exile.

I never met Edna for she had gone away before I was born. My mother had attended the same school, and sometimes Edna and her sisters would cycle out to my mother's farm to buy eggs or baby chickens. Like my mother, at the age of thirteen, Edna went away to boarding school, in her case at a convent in Loughrea, less than an hour's drive by hackney car, and then, at seventeen, she began to study in Dublin to become a pharmacist, something my mother had once dreamed of doing. Edna's name would come up at family gatherings, but I never paid much attention until suddenly, just before I went away to boarding school, she became famous when her novel *The Country Girls* was published in London.

I wouldn't have known of its success, or perhaps paid much attention, if it hadn't created a scandal and she herself became a story in the newspapers. The novel was instantly banned by the Irish Censorship Board, so nobody was allowed to read it in Ireland, although, in any case, mine was not a community of readers. My father found it easy to live without books for, in his view, news from the outside world was to be taken with a grain of salt; he believed that many dubious truths were peddled for somebody's gain. Even though he wasn't a great talker, spontaneous talk was normal in his world, and reading and writing were foreign – imported skills from a duplicitous other class that traded in secrets and codes. It was one way to maintain the certainty of local truths and convictions.

Edna's interviews in London, accompanied by photographs that revealed her to have a glamorous, film-star presence, were outspoken in their attacks on the clerical domination of Irish society, on repression, and hypocrisy. She spoke of how women suffered in such a rural society. I immediately got the impression that she was no longer a loyal Irish Catholic, and that writing had become an act of defiance for her. I was confused by what some considered to be an act of betrayal, and yet I was curious about this cousin of mine away in London.

Long before the end of each month, I went through the shelf of books that were delivered to the school. It didn't matter that the adventure stories had English or American heroes; I read to be taken away from the farm, to have the weight of my own imagination lifted. But now I wanted to read this other kind of book, a book that was banned and upset people.

I wanted to read Edna's book, for suddenly my attention was drawn to the notion that a book was something that might be written by a person one might know, whose real life had gone into the making of it.

What could be in *The Country Girls* that might be dangerous, from which we Irish should be protected? I asked my mother, and she told me that the book included characters Edna had copied from people in the town: they were clearly recognizable. So this was it. People would be embarrassed in front of their neighbours. Outsiders would look at the town with ridicule and suspicion. The town would be shamed by such self-consciousness.

But was it a true story? My mother could not tell me that since she hadn't read the book, but I was old enough to be told of an earlier scandal. Edna had "blotted her copybook" and had gone off to London to live after disgracing her family. Her father had been driven in a hackney car up to Wicklow, accompanied by a priest, to confront her in the house she lived in with an older man. They planned to force her to marry him, now that she was pregnant, but her father had failed to gain entry to the house.

So was this what the story was about? Such matters that any family would wish to keep secret had been turned into a public drama by her father's actions. And now she told secrets in print, shamelessly exposing her own immoral behaviour? All my mother knew was that Drewsboro House was in it, as was the farm worker who relieved himself in a pea tin and tossed the contents from his upstairs window over the hydrangeas. This sounded more like the stuff of jokes to me than a cause of scandal, and I wanted to read the book even more.

That Christmas, when we were leaving the house of a relative after an evening visit, I noticed my mother accepting a package wrapped in brown paper. One of the cousins of this family had once shared a flat with Edna in Dublin, where she worked in the bank. Sometimes she went to Belfast on the train for a day's shopping. I didn't know until later, when I went to university, that the Saturday day-trip over the border into British-controlled Northern Ireland was a way many Dubliners practised small subversions, won small freedoms: in Belfast, they could buy condoms, and other products not available in the Republic of Ireland, including banned books.

On the way home, I asked my mother what the package contained, and after I pestered her over and over, she revealed that it was a copy of *The Country Girls*. Naturally, I wanted to read it, but within a day or two, the brown-covered book was spirited out of the house. I never discovered what she thought of it or if she agreed with the action of the censors. I feel sure she did for in her mind the laws of the Church and of the State were one, and they were guardians of the minds of the people. I wondered if she felt that she was in a state of sinfulness even as she read it and had to confess her guilt later.

Already I felt certain I would read this book, whatever the risks to my immortal soul. The unexpected revelation that my cousin Edna was a published writer suddenly validated for me that private and deeply pleasurable world of reading that I had often thought was mere fantasy, a child's escapism that would be surrendered when I became a grown-up. Suddenly, books became not a private and eccentric pleasure but something dangerous and powerful that could frighten people, and, in addition, the writing of books was something that could be done by people I might know. My occasional fantasy that I would continue to read books into my adult life now became the fantasy that I might also write them.

*

Looking back fifty years to this time when childhood was ending, I believe the significance of Edna O'Brien in our local and national consciousness was due to an anxious awareness of concealed truths in many lives, and indeed to the unnerving idea of exposure. Privacy and "minding your own business" is one thing, but when I think back, past the public demonstrations of piety and jokiness, the necessary acting out of personal and communal control, and the sports, the dances, the music and fun, which are the stuff of country life, another current of interest connected to concealment and scandal appears to have been common, giving rise to both denial and fascination.

Why draw attention to Edna's novel on a national stage? Why not let it pass, letting it find its readers or not, as is the fate of so many books? Censorship and control are, of course, political imperatives, as they were behind the Iron Curtain in the Soviet Union and Eastern Europe — we knew this — but did the power of the Catholic Church really depend on censorship, or was its moral authority affirmed in the policing of "bad thoughts"? The secrecy of the confessional is at the heart of this issue, for it is there that the priest exercises God's authority to forgive sin or to withhold forgiveness and thus to determine the future of one's immortal soul. The naked truth about oneself — one's private behaviour, one's thoughts and beliefs — was confronted in the dark box with the priest listening behind the grill: it was indeed a frightening ritual for children or scrupulous adults, a ritual of stripping and punishment with the reward of blessing and sanctifying grace from on high. The truth was everything here: telling the whole list of sins, mortal and venial, and utter humiliation was called for, the fear of having missed out on any misdemeanour a cause of further anxiety and a guilty conscience.

If confessing the truth of one's own shameful nature in a dark box was the core of Catholic practice — and there were many people who went routinely every week, or month, others only fulfilling the absolute requirement of an annual good confession and communion at Eastertime — the notion of this kind of stripping and exposure of self was surely an unspoken part of the cultural fabric. The privileged secrecy of the confessional was maintained, for the priest had the absolute right and duty to be silent regarding the sins he was told when he acted as God's surrogate. Sins and secrecy; privileged knowledge for God's ears only and the hypocrisy of piety; this Catholic practice cultivated at once the mentality of scandal-seeking and denial. Ritual was everything, the intimate life of each individual contained in that black box, although, of course, the unspoken truth was that many individuals' secret experience of pleasure or pain, of instinctive behaviour, sometimes came to the attention of others only to be severely contained, or indeed ruthlessly punished with banishment or ostracization from the family. I knew of this intimately in my mother's family, for her mother had expelled her brother when his girlfriend had become pregnant, even though he had married her. And my mother had supported that expulsion, I realized, as I became aware of the absence of this uncle whom I had known earlier in childhood as pleasure-loving and fun to meet, and then as I grew older and asked about him, I learned that he and his wife and children – my cousins – lived a short distance away from my mother's home and that we passed the house regularly but never called in.

So much of this ethos gradually came into public view as the sexual and physical abuse of children by priests and religious authority figures in schools and orphanages became public knowledge in the nineties and after. The commissions of inquiry that investigated the extent of this abuse and reported back on the means used by Church authorities to conceal what they knew of the predator priests and abusers, mostly of boys, wrote a new social and cultural history of the twentieth century in Ireland. The intention was to bring into view what had been covered up, so that legal consequences would ensue for predators, and the victimized would be compensated; more than this, their testimony was acknowledged as truth, and the efforts made to silence them or deny their intimate experience was seen to be as much a general cultural phenomenon as the work of devious authority figures.

An aspect of this new awareness that strikes me is that, looking back, one can identify many individuals on the margins of the rural society, the men often notable as heavy drinkers, the women reclusive or odd, and one wonders what secret histories might be written about these individuals. The aura of a pointless or wasted life, a life that somehow never reached any satisfactory purpose, enveloped them in their eccentric separateness.

★

One of the few books in our house was an old medical textbook. It had belonged to one of the O'Brien cousins, Martin, who had been cared for by my paternal grandmother, and it was she who had sent him to Dublin to study Medicine. Its illustrations had given me my first inklings about the differences between the bodies of men and women and how babies are born, but equally interesting were the slogans about the 1916 Rising which were written on the flyleaves, for Martin had been in the centre of Dublin in that year. He had not joined the Rising, although he or someone had written "Up the Republic" and "Eire Abu" on the book with a thick blue pencil, nor did he become a doctor. Instead, it appears, he had literally gone to the dogs, had spent his time and money at the Harold's Cross track for greyhound racing and had failed to pass his first-year exams.

But Martin's interest in the dogs did not end with gambling on the evening's races while he was in Dublin. In a way, they became his life. He became the owner and trainer of greyhounds and had major success with some of them, including winning the Cup at Clounanna, the premier coursing event of the year. Coursing is a country version of what happens in the stadium, using a live hare rather than a mechanical one, and racing just two dogs at a time. Coursing was a very popular wintertime sport in the counties around Clare: Galway, Tipperary, Limerick. My uncle Willie, who farmed the other half of the original farm that my grandparents split between my father and him, also had greyhounds, and I often accompanied my retired aunt to the coursing meetings, where Willie and Martin O'Brien, bachelors, about fifty years old, would meet up. My aunt was there to bring home the dogs after the event so that Martin and Willie could tour their favourite watering holes, and it was often the case that their bachelor celebrations might continue for a few days. This lifestyle also included trips to the race meetings in Limerick and Galway, and, indeed, when I went to my uncle's house, I would sometimes see the two cousins with the sporting pages spread out double on the kitchen table as they prepared their bets before setting off to the bookies' office in Scariff. There would be high excitement in the air at the prospects for the day. My uncle would tease me and my brother, urging us to grow up to emulate a famous pair of jockeys at this time, the Taaffe brothers, but I knew well that my mother and father did not approve of this dissolute lifestyle.

One of the turning points of my growing up concerns Martin O'Brien and took place in the summer of my twelfth year. He had been spending more and more time at my uncle's house, leaving his unmarried brother and sister to take care of the farm all three had inherited. He would sometimes come to our house and my father and he would share a whiskey or two and engage in inconsequential conversation. Martin would never accompany my father fishing, and the visits seemed to be no more than nostalgic, a return to the house where he had spent some of his childhood years. I thought of him distantly as a bachelor countryman in unkempt clothes, tweed jacket and overcoat, dirty, unironed shirts always worn with a tie, unpolished leather shoes, who drove a battered blue van, and whose real life was somehow undefined, apart from drinking and gambling.

That summer, to everyone's amazement, the news emerged that Willie had married in Dublin while attending the All-Ireland hurling final. His secret wedding did not include Martin, nor did he return home with his wife, someone he had known, apparently, for many years in one of his favourite pubs in Tipperary, owned by her family. The routine life of the house continued for some time, my retired aunt, Willie, and Martin living together with my grandmother, and they continued to train the greyhounds for the coursings. The mystery of my uncle's sexual life – if that was what it was – remained until my aunt revealed to us that Willie was about to become a father. It was still not clear if his wife would remain with the child in her home place or would join her husband. The baby was born, and then it was announced that mother and son would be joining the household in a week.

A few days before the arrival, my aunt appeared one morning in our yard to enquire if we had seen Martin. We had not. She had not seen him since the previous evening, he had not slept in the house, and his blue van was there. Probably on the assumption that he might have had a heart attack, my father immediately set out to walk the fields between the two houses. He found nothing and on his return set off for the lakeshore. He brought me with him and remarked that Martin might have taken out the boat. We checked the boathouse and found everything normal, and then my father made a remark that puzzled me. He said we would walk the shore to see if we might find his cap. Much of the foreshore had bushes down to the water's edge, and so we had to struggle to make our way towards Williamstown, beating back briars and juniper trees as we went. My father said nothing as we worked, but I sensed his anxiety. We found nothing.

Later in the evening, my aunt returned to tell us that Martin's body had been found by the postman returning home, hanging from a tree at the far end of Willie's farm. The body was taken down and hidden in the garage until such time as it could be arranged for an ambulance to transport it to the morgue at the local hospital. I knew from the remarks I overheard that the true cause of his death was being concealed, and a story was made up to explain it. No contact was made with the local priest until the body had been taken to the hospital because it was known that burial in the graveyard would be refused if the true circumstances of his death were known. The sin of despair, this final abandonment of belief in God's mercy, or in prayer as a means of salving all suffering, placed the person outside of the sacraments of the Church. This was the opposite of the "deathbed conversions" and "baptisms of desire" that teachers of Christian doctrine made so much of, the happy endings after all, the expressions of faith.

I have often wondered about the secret history of Martin O'Brien's despair, and indeed how much of his life had been spent evading or postponing this final decision. What role did alcohol play? Or his addiction to gambling, if it can be said that this man's preference for the excitement of the chase over any profession or job, over helping out on his own farm even, can be called that. When I questioned my mother much later, she told me that he was a depressed man who often retired to bed and refused to leave his house for periods during his life. His brother and sister took care of him. I had not known this and simply remembered him as someone who came and went irregularly, although I had found it odd that he appeared to have moved into Willie's house more or less permanently in the last years of his life. Towards the end of her life, when we returned to the topic, my mother revealed that Martin had been on medication for some time, and that my aunt had advised him to stop taking it. What the benefits of the medication were, or what the side effects might have been, my mother did not know.

Nowadays I wonder if he suffered from a form of depression that might have been managed properly if the investigation of mental illness was not enveloped in ignorance and superstition. Did he have bipolar disorder, as the cyclical binges of high excitement and withdrawal to passivity may suggest? I also wonder if he might have been gay, knowingly or unknowingly. It is likely that he knew of my uncle's secret sexual life, for I discovered later that he had been sexually active before his late marriage. One of the maids, who took care of him and his mother before my aunt retired, had become pregnant. But I wondered about Martin's attachment to his cousin and the timing of his suicide.

I will never know the answers to such speculations regarding the secrets and repressions of these country people in a closed, Church-dominated culture, but I feel sure that the impact of these events on me was major. More than the scandalous novel of Edna O'Brien, this suicide made me reflect on how all of us have secret lives, and how our burden of shame or despair may lead, unknown to anyone, towards such an end. More than anything, Martin O'Brien's frightening action had conveyed to me a new truth: that our life is not always in God's hands but in our own. It is the truth the Church could not admit, and one that I could only fully admit to myself later as adolescent pessimism grew and I moved towards abandonment of everything Catholicism professed. Our life is in our own hands, to give or to take, and even though I found support for my explorations of such thoughts in places like Camus's *The Myth of Sisyphus*, the burden of carrying responsibility for one's own life is a major challenge, sometimes overwhelming and paralyzing, depressing indeed; and one realization that comes out of the challenge is that for most people the release offered by religious belief is a welcome one. Another realization is that when one can join one's life in love to another person, as I was lucky to do, one learns that daily choices, the smallest gestures of giving a part of one's life to another person every day, to one's spouse or children or grandchildren, a friend, or an unknown person, is the greatest affirmation one can have that our life is actually ours to give.

*

All these events created the enveloping culture that embedded in me attitudes towards sex and self-esteem, confession, guilt and shame, transgression and punishment – the small events in an individual's life and the attitudes that permeate the exercise of authority in a particular society. And all this enveloping culture closed in on me in the aftermath of incidents of sexual abuse by a workman on our farm. It was my own secret scandal, something unknown to my parents and brother. These incidents happened without violence in the year before I went away to the monks' school for boys, and it was only there that I entered the black box of confession and felt I should confess the sexual habit I had slipped into as a result.

It was during a retreat given by priests of the Passionist order, three days of silence and prayer, sermons and meditation that all us boys had to undergo. Something a priest said about our bodies as "Temples of the Holy Ghost" had at first seemed like an extravagant metaphor, but his angry words took on a more physical aura when the sin of "self-abuse" was mentioned.

It led me to think about my habit, for what the workman had done to me awakened sexual sensations that I could explore myself, and I did. Now, this atmosphere of pervasive sinfulness was designed to make us examine our consciences: in what way had we perverted God's plan? In what ways had we committed mortal or venial sins? We must prepare for a general confession and put our whole past life of sins behind us forever. We must cleanse ourselves and look forward to a life of purity and grace.

I was twelve years old, in my first year, and the language of the missioners was carefully suggestive so that it gave no ideas to anyone who had no ideas before but planted a thought in the minds of those like myself who might indeed join some dots. Nobody had ever told me the facts of life, neither my parents nor anyone else, although later one of the priests would take me aside for a private walk and discussion. I had picked up some biological and anatomical ideas in Martin O'Brien's medical textbook and from observing the bull and the cows and reproduction in other animals on the farm. I had little information with which to understand what this man was doing to me or even to consider it a grievous violation. But now in the hours of silence and meditation, I began to feel that "self-abuse" might refer to what I was doing.

On the last day of the retreat, I entered the confessional and broached the subject of my sin to the priest. I was right to have heard anger in his words for now his anger was directed at me. He told me I had committed a mortal sin and if I did not stop this activity I would go to hell. There was no doubt about it. He enquired a little about the circumstances and I told him about the workman. He expressed little interest. He did not appear to think that this man had done anything wrong or that his actions were the mortal sins, not mine. The priest was singularly interested in my sin, and I was left thinking it was the greatest sin I could commit, and that even at this early stage of my life and in a state of such ignorance, I was profoundly guilty. I felt sentenced to death, to eternal damnation, and when he gave me absolution and a rosary for penance, it felt like a lucky break, a stay of execution.

The shock of this event in the black box has stayed with me all my life, the extent of its devastation obviously greatest in the days, months, and years following. It was rarely out of my mind, and I struggled to understand and accept what had taken on such far-reaching personal consequences. Disbelief and unreality jostled with shame and guilt, and as I inevitably slipped back into my habit, further confessions reinforced the shock of the first. My naturally scrupulous character, my shyness, my sense of being special in my mother's eyes now turned into another way of being special, a secret sinner trapped in the hypocrisy of being an exemplary good boy in the school, a high achiever, a model conformist. Everything in my adolescent years was a deception as I craved approval and acceptance, and strove to win them, for in my own mind I had to conquer my own sinful nature and my worthlessness in the eyes of God. Everything to do with sex was double-sided, my instincts already branded as sinful and leading me towards damnation, so many situations occasions of sin, and my fellow teenagers were so eager for adventures with girls while I awkwardly struggled with my contradictions and my secret shame. This continued until I was able to defy God and priests and the whole notion of sinfulness, and begin to accept my body as my own and take my life as a freedom rather than a guilty burden. But that would only come to me through various kinds of rebellion and over many years.

What strikes me now as extraordinary is that "self-abuse" was considered by these priests to be a mortal sin that could lead to eternal damnation, but during all those years, nobody in my experience even mentioned abuse or abuser. The absence of these key words for aggression and violation reflects the absence of even a way of thinking or talking about such things. While this is an aspect of a general censorship mentality regarding all sexual behaviour, a kind of taboo, it still remains hard to grasp the mindset of those who blame the victim, or encourage the victim to blame himself or herself, and hard to believe that the absence of a few simple words could reflect and support that culture. And yet the entry of those words into general discourse has had the effect of a cultural revolution.

*

On holidays I would hear stories of Edna O'Brien. The parish priest had burned a copy of *The Country Girls*, and her mother had destroyed it too. New novels appeared almost every year, all of them banned in Ireland, and so I could not know that she was writing the further adventures of Kate and Baba as they grew from country girls into married women in London where exiled bliss was grim and bitter. The newspapers carried stories of Edna as a celebrity taking part in the Aldermaston March and other Ban the Bomb activities, appearing in early television debates on abortion, hobnobbing with celebrated writers like Harold Pinter, and promoting an agenda of women's issues. At first all this was beyond my ability to grasp; seen from the monks' school for boys, she lived in another world and her preoccupations seemed crazed and eccentric.

During these years of adolescence, however, I grew into someone who wanted to be a reader of the silences that envelop so many lives. I wanted to know not only the sexual secrets that all adolescents cannot wait to discover, but also the secret of why some people are driven to live a certain kind of life, especially a life in which respectability and conventional status are thrown to the wind. Edna has such a life, and she became my first model of the writer who deliberately tells secrets, who expands the boundaries of what may be told.

One night at the end of library period, the supervising priest, Fr. Bernard, held up a book he had just confiscated from one of the boys and went into a tirade about unsuitable books. This particular book was by an Irishman named Joyce; even though he was a Catholic, he was an enemy of the faith. He had written dirty books that were banned everywhere in the world. He had used books to plant immoral thoughts in people's minds; in other words, he had made reading an occasion of sin. He took something that was for a good purpose and perverted it. But God had punished him for his mortal sins by giving him a horrible disease called syphilis. His mind had rotted away and he had died a most painful death.

When we came out of the study hall, one of my friends broke into a mocking laugh. He knew that Bernie had told us lies about James Joyce. It was not true that he had died of syphilis. And his novel about growing up could be bought anywhere. It wasn't banned, nor was his book of stories, *Dubliners*. The copy of *A Portrait of the Artist as a Young Man*, which Bernie had held up in rage, was the orange-coloured Penguin edition.

We were all free to read it.

In the days following, we dared each other with a scary plan: to order books directly from Penguin in England. We could club together and order whatever we'd like to read. We could order *A Portrait* and *1984,* which our English teacher told us about. Someone said it was banned, and then we wondered what would happen if we ordered banned books. Would the customs officers open the parcel? I suddenly had an idea: this would be the way to get a copy of *The Country Girls,* for I knew that it had come out in Penguin paperback.

The parcel would come into the college under the gaze of the priests. Should we risk that, for the consequences of being caught would certainly be expulsion from the college? We might destroy our whole school career and our future prospects, and the scandal would disgrace our parents. After all, importing banned books into Ireland was a criminal act.

Our rebellion, our need to defy the authority of priests who had lost our respect, was desperate enough that we decided to risk it. Some weeks later, at the end of lunch one day, the priest read out as usual the names of boys who had received a parcel, the monthly stock of goodies from home for the tuck box that many boys kept in a locked room near the kitchen. Among the names was mine. What was going to happen when I went to the President's room to pick up the parcel? Would the priest be suspicious and open the box? Would he know which books were banned?

So good had I been through all the years here, so successful in winning honour for the college, with never a hint of rebellion, that I passed under the radar. I found the parcel and walked out of the President's office carrying my bomb, my box of scandalous books that might prove dangerous to our faith and morals, even if we escaped expulsion. We might be about to destroy our peace of mind forever by discovering the secrets that had caused these books to be banned. We all knew that we had created an occasion of sin for each other, for we were all Children of Mary, but the excitement of anticipation had a mysterious sexual thrill — the thrill of defiance and of surrendering to impulse.

The Country Girls disappointed me for there were no secrets — and no sex — as far as I could see. It was hard to see what had been so shocking. The two adolescent girls were funny and sad and silly. There was some frankness and irreverence, and I could recognize in a vague way that Edna had been inspired by her village, for the novel was set in such a country place. But it seemed too simple to satisfy my hunger. I didn't feel any enlargement of self, scandalous or otherwise.

Maybe the fuss was about the fact that girls hadn't been written about in this way already. I remembered something Edna had said in the papers about the freedom women needed to live their own lives. Was it possible that the censor had wanted to keep these high-spirited rogues hidden in case girls who read the book would become rebellious in turn, and maybe much more so? My own need was so great that a revolutionary act would have to be loudly proclaimed; this first novel of Edna O'Brien told secrets that shocked some people, but to me it seemed surprisingly tame in its depiction of desperation.

Joyce's *Portrait* was far more disturbing. Although Edna's book had captured the world of my childhood, when Joyce wrote of Clongowes and Belvedere I felt he was describing the mentality and ethos of my own school. Much more than *The Country Girls*, the style of the book had an atmosphere of certainty and confidence in exploring the very things that were troubling me. When he wrote of Stephen's religious doubts and his striving for intellectual certainty, it was as if he was describing me.

Joyce made it seem inevitable that as you became more educated and could understand more about life, you would cast off the prohibition against thinking that the priests and the Church wanted to impose. Stephen was a young man who wanted to be free in his mind to follow his own thoughts to their logical end. Wasn't that what education was supposed to be for? How could the priests hope to defend themselves against that, especially with ignorant attacks like Bernie's wild speech in the study hall? Bernie had appeared contemptible, whereas Stephen Dedalus was admirable. He had made the goal of his life the free and honest search for understanding, whatever the cost. His rebellion had carried him out of the darkness of home and school and into a world of knowledge and art.

I wasn't clear what Stephen's sexual sins were and how he had escaped from shame and guilt. It didn't seem to be the important thing, for Stephen's confidence and power came from his intellectual supremacy. In that way, I would become like Stephen Dedalus.

*

Long before the commissions of enquiry into sexual abuse were set up, a novel had given great insight into the ethos that was documented a generation later. Naturally, the book was banned, and I did not read it until I came to Canada. The novel was *The Dark* by John McGahern. Published in 1965, it is a brief, impassioned portrait of an adolescent boy who is terrorized by his father and sexually abused. His mother has died, and he remembers how she had loved him. The unnamed boy masturbates regularly and struggles with his guilty conscience. A priest who craves intimacy and affection comes to his bed at night; a sister is sexually molested by her employer; the country landscape is bleak and inhospitable. The boy struggles to recover some self-esteem through his academic talent, and dreams of the empowerment that university will give him, but the novel's exploration of the darkness that envelops him ends in a revelation of how his will has been eroded. McGahern was fired from his teaching position when the novel was banned, and he left Ireland to find work.

I was now old enough to know that McGahern's art and the evolution of his style were things I wanted to reflect on, but I also found myself wondering about the secret histories of others who had left Ireland. How often were their leave-takings not undertaken for economic reasons? Many may have chosen exile because they had been abused, repressed or shamed, and they had to escape their daily life in Ireland, which would constantly reinforce the burden of anguish they carried in secret. I wondered of how many this might be said. Surely it was not only writers like Edna O'Brien and John McGahern who had been compelled to leave or stay away? And how many found in exile the means to free themselves from their past? So much history has been written of Irish emigration and "the diaspora," but it is only in a handful of memoirs that I have seen any effort to consider that economic or political models of dispossession and destitution may not tell the whole story.

FOUR

My first "foreign" country was the Aran Islands, and now that I am giving a shape to these feelings of attachment and estrangement, I imagine that they may have first surfaced during the weeks I spent on Inishere in my eleventh summer. It was my teacher's belief that I should spend a month in an Irish College, and he contrived a situation so that I could get a small scholarship. A new college had been set up on the smallest of the Irish-speaking islands off the coast of Clare, and the organizers offered a scholarship to each National School in the county. His contrivance for our school was a lottery, but I feel certain that he wanted me to win, as the one in our small school who was most likely to come back with a *blas*, an authentic speaker of Irish. I would be keen, he knew, and I was going to be sent away to boarding school to continue my education at second level, and maybe I would go on to become a teacher. And for that I would have to be fluent in Irish and to believe in the "national language." I would join the many young people who made the summer trip to the west of Ireland, to stay for a month with native-speaking families and to be absorbed in their daily life and culture. He could never have imagined how his effort to have me immersed led to a very unexpected awakening to another culture and way of life, not at all the one he had wished for.

Inishere is only sixty miles away from the farm as the crow flies, just a short distance out in the Atlantic ocean from the

Clare coast, but it was at this time, 1959, an entirely isolated community with certain modern amenities but still living an elemental life of self-supporting work. The men fished and hauled seaweed from the shore to fertilize little gardens between the rocks in which they grew potatoes and cabbage. These plots were protected from the Atlantic storms and the harsh salt winds by high stone walls, so that the side of the island that was inhabited, close to the mainland, was a maze of narrow lanes between these small cultivated patches. The women had spinning wheels and from the spun yarn they made almost all their own clothes – heavy tweed trousers and skirts to the ankle and knitted sweaters. The colours were always grey or navy blue, so that the small community on the island, perhaps three hundred, really did look like a community. On their feet they wore *pampooties*, shoes made from cow or seal skin. They didn't speak any English, they didn't read, and the only times anyone left the island were to go to hospital in Galway or to emigrate to America where they would join other islanders who had gone before them.

I stayed with a family called Seoighe, which they told me was Joyce in English, and even in this first gesture, I think I sensed their feeling of being divided or marginal. They were friendly and welcoming, gentle, but somewhat in awe of a boy from the mainland. They found it hard to imagine the size of our farm, the number of cows and cattle and all the animals that lived on it. But for me their island was a storybook place with a ruined Norman castle, a recent large shipwreck, caves and beaches, and, at the deserted Atlantic side, a lighthouse where I was welcomed by the keeper and brought to the top to see how it worked. This was a boy's heaven. It was summertime, and apart from some classes, and *céilí* dancing and music in the evenings, I was free to roam and explore for hours every day. I was in a foreign country, experiencing for the first time another language and another culture, but in many ways it was only a backdrop for other things. Equally strange to me was the foreign country of adolescence. I felt alone and apart from the gangs of older boys and girls, especially the mixed ones, who wandered all over the island. They were from small towns around the county and seemed to have a sense of *savoir faire* that left me feeling awkward and ill at ease. For the first time, I felt isolated from my peers. I was an onlooker at their communal lives, threatened by their spontaneous play, their tense laughter, their constant excited talk. I sensed the confident or risky play of adolescent energies, the bravado, the flirting, the rivalries, the performances and the attention seeking. It was my first time away from home, and I kept to myself.

One evening, soon after I arrived, I was walking alone and met a middle-aged American couple. They were talkative, asked me about myself, and told me that they were just coming to the end of a long stay on the island, living among the islanders. They described themselves and the work they did in a word I had never heard and could not repeat. They were anthropologists, and suddenly I became aware of the island culture that I was supposed to absorb as my native inheritance from a new distance: as an object of strangeness and curiosity for people from far away, from America. I was struck by the idea of such a profession of observation and note-taking, and I sometimes think that this passing contact may have awakened in me, or reinforced tendencies already nascent, a sense of how a certain kind of close observation could be a way of life, a way of understanding and accumulating knowledge.

While this notion that I was awakened to such an idea of life, or even of academic life, as a researcher, may be far-fetched in a boy of eleven from the country, something confirms the idea. I kept a brief record of my time on Inishere, which I still have. It is not simply a photograph album with "snaps" of the family, or a diary of my doings, although at first glance it may seem no more than that, but it has a hint of detachment, of my attempt to study the culture I found, to present an account that reflects an overview, a rudimentary ethnography. Extraordinarily, the experience on Inishere, in my first other culture, seems to have been one during which I learned not to immerse myself, not to take on an identity through imitation, but to detach myself through observation and description. It may have been the encounter with the Messengers, or my reading in Classics Illustrated of Stanley's search for Livingstone, or it may, indeed, have been my own isolation among the tribal gangs of adolescents which made me an onlooker and reinforced a sense of ambiguity about the whole question of identity and belonging.

More surprising still on the island was my discovery of "The Dane," a weaver of colourful woollen belts on a large handloom he had built for himself. Unlike the anthropologists, he appeared to live alone and apart from the islanders, even though he had settled there almost ten years before, in the post-war years. He lived in a small stone house in a sandy hollow behind the beach, away from the villages that had formed in sheltered pockets under the central hill. He had a small kitchen and slept in a loft overhead. His furnishings, his clothing, his food were all basic – monastic. In this, his style was not so different from the islanders' own simplicity, as if he had grasped the opportunity this environment gave him to strip away all the inessentials of modern life.

He welcomed visitors to his workshop, for he would talk as he worked, and he gradually began to tell me stories of his life in Copenhagen before the war and then in the resistance during the Nazi occupation. I was fascinated and went back almost every day. He was a reader and had a small collection of books – he loaned me *The Colditz Story* – and he was also a painter. Next to his workshop he had set up a small gallery. It was my first gallery and my discovery of painting as an art, although I could hardly respond to the small oil paintings, in the style of Cézanne. The whitewashed walls gleamed behind the small canvases of still lifes in vibrant colours. The Dane painted little now, although he showed me reviews in the newspapers of a successful exhibition in Dublin before he moved to the island. And before that he had spent some time in a Benedictine monastery in England. I knew in some vague way that he was a refugee from the barbarism of the war-years, a searcher for some peace and simplicity, but he seemed to have no wish to learn Irish or to integrate himself into the community.

My few weeks on Inishere left me with so many impressions of life and different ways of thinking about it that I learned little Irish, and my young self absorbed much that may have shaped me in my future life away. Rather than become more rooted in my native culture, I became more estranged, more ready to think of myself as a traveller, as a searcher, as an observer.

★

I might have grown into an outsider in any case, whatever the family history or the name, because my mother had aspirations for me, and they would be realized through education. In particular, she was keen that I learn French. It may have been her love of cooking that started her dream of the refinement of French culture, for she did not know the language and had not travelled there, even as a pilgrim to Lourdes. At any rate, she was pleased when the woman she had found to give me piano lessons, an old retired lady in a home run by a French order of nuns, turned out to have spent her entire life in France. Miss Gretta Geoghegan, a convent-educated lady from Carlow, had become a governess before World War I and had lived with many different families in various parts of France, and then moved to San Sebastian when the Nazis invaded. I was nine, and began piano lessons with her, but soon my mother asked her to give me French lessons too.

I remember sitting in the dining room of the home in the next village, Mountshannon, looking down the lawn to the lake, for it had once been a hotel, while Miss Geoghegan went on for hours about the Marquis de Something and the Comtesse de Something Else, and she mentioned towns and châteaux, and who was related to whom in the French aristocracy, until the sounds of the language became familiar to my ears. From time to time we returned to the lesson. My textbook was *Assimil: French without Toil*. I think I may have brought hope into her life as she sank into this retirement of obscurity, without any family relation, it seemed, in Ireland, which she hadn't visited during her forty years away. Maybe she imagined that I might become a young gentleman like one of her French boys. And so as I cycled after school up and down the hills between the farm and the Bon Secours Home in Mountshannon, repeating my French verbs, practising my French *r*'s and *u*'s, it was easy for me to imagine myself on a *route* somewhere between a château and a vineyard.

It was in the boarding school that I came into contact with the other *blas*, the correct French accent. I had a bad-tempered teacher for whom none of us could do anything right. Only now do I recognize that he was at the mercy of perfection, and most likely his spoken French had been subjected to correction in France. Miss Geoghegan had, over the decades of living in France, come to speak the language impeccably and without self-consciousness. At any rate, she had encouraged me to fall in love with French, and this difficulty had not surfaced. Soon I became aware of the high standard, the almost impossible standard expected by native French speakers, and the realization grew that no matter how much immersion or effort, I would never reach the state of cultural beatification represented by a Parisian *blas*.

*

My first journey out of Ireland was to France.

I did not go on a pilgrimage to the shrine of Our Lady of Lourdes in the Pyrenees, which was the only part of France that anyone we knew in Clare had ever been to. Groups of pilgrims, chaperoned by priests, travelled overland to have their Catholicism of apparitions, miracle cures, and rosaries reaffirmed in one of the major sites of such belief. They came back with bottles of Lourdes water, medals, statues, and transparent plastic globes with "snow" inside that fell gently over the miniature statue of the Virgin Mary. There were other sites of French sainthood that we knew of, such as Lisieux, where the miracles at the convent of Sainte Thérèse, the "Little Flower," took place. In school we had heard fragments of historical information about France, Louis XIV, *le Roi-Soleil*, and the Napoleonic wars, but it was as a Catholic country that France was known to us, the place where Irish priests had been trained during the persecution of Catholics in the eighteenth century and where the old Gaelic chieftains, the "Wild Geese," flew into exile a century earlier.

What I did in 1964 was unheard of: a boy from a farm in the West of Ireland went off to spend six weeks with a French family, flying from Shannon Airport to Le Bourget, north of Paris. I did not go to have my faith affirmed, or my Irishness, the two main concerns of our community discourse and educational system, and I'm sure my mother never thought my going would disturb any such scaffoldings of identity. She believed wholeheartedly in giving me the best opportunities she could afford for my education, my preparation for a highly successful career, in the way she could imagine it. This frustrated farmer's wife, who had high ambitions for her son, never dreamed that France might encourage thoughts of a liberation from that place in ways she could never articulate and might even live to regret.

I could not articulate them myself either, for both of us were in thrall to an idea of ambition and qualifications, most concretely a high position in the civil service, but enveloping this goal was a dream of fulfilment, of cultural enlargement of self which my mother associated with travel. She was frustrated in her own educational and career goals by an old-fashioned father who agreed to send her away to boarding school, as her aunt, a nun, had urged, but then cut the process short at age sixteen, after she had achieved high results in her Intermediate Certificate examinations. It was 1934, and all he could imagine was to bring her home so that she would eventually marry a local farmer, but she already had dreams.

The dreams survived in a way for they came alive when she spotted opportunities for me. One summer, the nuns at the home in Mountshannon asked her if a boy from France could come to stay with us to learn English. It would be an exchange, so that the following summer I would go to stay with his family in Pontoise, a town not far from Paris where the nuns had another community. Her answer was an unhesitant yes. Patrice Farge, my first Frenchman, spent six weeks with us, and I remember trying to imagine what he might be thinking of the place he had arrived in, how strange and foreign it must be to him, how different, although I could not imagine where he came from, nor articulate a sense of difference. All I knew was country and city, for I had cousins in the city who sometimes came to the farm, and I had visited them in Dublin, but Patrice communicated little about where he came from or where he thought he was. He clearly appreciated much of the farm life and activities, from helping to save the hay to fishing with my father, to my mother's baking and wholesome food.

I became aware again of accent, rather than vocabulary, as the decisive feature of speaking a foreign language. When Patrice spoke his first words in English, I noted his French way of pronouncing the language that he was attempting to use with an Oxbridge or BBC accent. Clearly, this was what was required of him at school, and suddenly I was aware of our farm dialect of English, heavily shadowed by the Gaelic that had been spoken in County Clare until a few generations before.

Suddenly, language was self-consciousness, the old sensitivities of class and power embedded in British-Irish distinctions were reflected in accents, but this had nothing to do with him. If I feared for what this language-learner from France might pick up, I was really feeling the doubts about identity and place that his presence aroused in me. Who was I in relation to someone outside my received cultural and historical moulds? What was the appropriate voice of the self?

My doubts survived and surfaced when I landed at Le Bourget a year later. Patrice was not there to meet me because he hadn't finished his exams at the Université de Grenoble, where he had gone to study Law. This disquieting news I gleaned from his younger brother Hervé, who had come to the airport with Madame Farge. He managed a few slow words in English, I a few words in French, but when they spoke to each other, I failed utterly to isolate a word from the flow. I was terrified by the speed and intonation of Madame Farge, which seemed to mirror the decisive and passionate way she drove the *deux-chevaux* once we began our journey across suburbs and small towns of Seine et Oise, the erratic dashes up and down streets and across roads without hedges or ditches that cut through immense cultivated fields, sudden stops at intersections, and last-minute swerves to another lane, which often resulted in fiery exchanges with other drivers or between mother and son. I had never thought of driving as an exercise of power, but the energetic authority of Madame's driving was soon reflected in the voice I heard orchestrating events in the kitchen as she and the maid prepared dinner.

Monsieur Farge emerged from his *cabinet*, a slight, somewhat abstracted lawyer of at least seventy years of age.

Most of the ground floor of this tall house on a cobbled street in the old town was a waiting room and office. The dining room table was set with a white tablecloth to the floor. I was presented with my own serviette and ring. Maître Farge sat at the head of the table, and the serving dish for each course came to him first. They tried conversation with me, asking if I liked the soup, would I like a glass of wine, but soon gave up. Later, we moved to his sitting room behind his office where he smoked strong-smelling cigarettes, holding the cigarette in his mouth as he spoke so that it seemed to smoulder into his wispy moustache. He read *Le Figaro* and *Le Monde* and offered commentaries to Hervé and Madame Farge in what seemed to be a bad-tempered and affronted tone. The news of the day seemed to frustrate him, and one day, when he decided to give me a lesson on pronunciation, it struck me that maybe his legal work with principles and precedents gave him an idea of perfection in all things that I and the world ought to match.

Everything was French, everything part of the texture of strangeness that I could observe but not really interpret. I soon realized that in this classically bourgeois French household – conservative, Catholic, Gaullist, as I would come to think of it in retrospect – my polite and deferential presentation of myself was exactly right. I accepted and appreciated everything, even, memorably, my first olives, which a caring lady at a garden party the next day kept passing to me, although I wished I could say no. I felt I was an object of curiosity at the party, still silent, still at sea. At the weekend, Patrice returned, just in time for the arrival of the whole family for the *fiançaille*, the engagement party, of his older brother Yves to Arlette. The part I was expected to play was clear, and I played it well; inhibition had prepared me well for this, suppressing as best I could feelings of shame, bewilderment, and awe, hoping that in time I would actually be worthy of my place in such a proper French home.

Whenever I see one of Monet's paintings of the Gare Saint-Lazare, I am back in the station we arrived at each day from Pontoise on our outings to the city. My encyclopaedia of France was already being written. I was good at remembering names, kings and painters, dates, historical events and movements, visual images and geographical locations. We went to the tourist spots, of course, *la tour Eiffel*, Notre-Dame, les Invalides, la Sainte-Chapelle, le Louvre, and up the hill to Montmartre and Sacré-Cœur. I bought postcards of all of them, dutifully followed the guides and read Patrice's *Guide Michelin*. He was my serious and earnest instructor in the official version of what was worth seeing in Paris, and I was his eager student. We went farther afield, to Versailles and Fontainebleau on day trips, to Chantilly, and I can clearly remember a short afternoon drive to Auvers-sur-Oise where we visited the grave of Vincent van Gogh.

Paris was my first imperial city, a city that reached beyond itself as the main site of French culture for the export of images of the history and heritage of la France. According to Patrice, it was a city that had to be mastered, an experience that had to be converted into knowledge. And so I learned also a way of approaching a city, a French way, not through its sounds, smells, styles, and people on the streets, its present state, but through its accumulated cultural wealth.

Patrice's encyclopaedic approach extended to another part of the country. His family had a summer house in a small village in Haute-Savoie on Lac Léman. The water of the small harbour lapped against the walls of the house beneath the balcony, a handful of sailboats drifted against the backdrop of the Swiss foothills between Geneva and Lausanne. The sun was intense, close to forty degrees Celsius, and this undeveloped village, a short distance from the celebrated spas of Évian-les-Bains and Thonon-les-Bains, was still as a dream, a picturesque place that had remained undisturbed since the nineteenth century. At school, I had memorized stanzas of Lamartine's poem on this lake, thinking it Wordsworthian in its feeling for the spiritual realities of nature, but the Farges smiled at the poem's extravagant romanticism when I mentioned it, and now I discovered that the Shelleys had lived here at the time that Mary had conceived of *Frankenstein*.

The place was altogether too quiet, or too claustrophobic, for Patrice and so he borrowed the *deux-chevaux,* and we set off on an Alpine tour that took us down to Annecy and on to Grenoble, skirting Mont Blanc, and then high into the Alps to his cousins' apartment in the ski resort of Deux Alpes. We took a ski lift to a level where snow and melting glaciers still lay in permanently shadowed corners, and hiked down with mountain views so steep that we felt safer sitting and sliding down grassy sections. The long circle back from Deux Alpes brought us first into Italy, to Torino, then north to the Grand St. Bernard Pass and into Switzerland, and then through the valley of Martigny to the lake and back by the spas to Nernier. I learned how to read the Michelin maps that guided our driving — a skill that would be essential later on my marathon drives in Canada and the Eastern United States. But I could tell that those Michelin maps and guidebooks were transmitting to me something else that was part of Patrice's conviction that nature itself could be civilized and made part of French culture.

Later, at university, I felt I should specialize in French, but soon realized that my stay in France had given me only a particular kind of enthusiasm; I did not have an intimate command of the grammar of the language that would allow me to excel academically. In spite of my ability to toss around names and the constant augmenting of my private encyclopaedia, I really had no special talent for the language or the culture. I could never be a mimic or translate myself into a Frenchman. All I had was a certain ease about speaking and reading the language; it no longer felt like a foreign tongue, and in a small way it had become part of me.

I gave up the study of French, but France had become part of my displacement in some other, more pivotal, way. In early 1969, I stayed with Patrice in the apartment in Paris he now shared with Hervé. My Paris on this occasion was not the museums but the streets where the revolution had happened the previous May. I hung around the Sorbonne, and up and down the Boulevard Saint-Michel, and Patrice brought me to the bar at the Cité universitaire where we could chat to students who had taken part in the street demonstrations. I even travelled out to Nanterre, the bleak modern campus in the suburbs where Danny the Red had established his base, and spent a day wandering around, deciphering the slogans on the walls, unsure if I was observing the ugly aftermath of a war or simply the uncollected garbage in an underfunded school. I was still looking for a France that would enlarge me, but I never did have the romantic encounter or the sexual initiation of the mythic France. The student revolution was another version of vague desire, and when I returned to Dublin I was inspired with ambitions to express my own revolutionary fantasies, which I did in street marches and in an "occupation" at the university.

*

I realize now that there were reasons why I did not pick up the Irish *blas* on Inishere, or the Parisian *b'as* in France. Or any authentic voice in another language. Maybe I have a poor ear for the music of accent, or lack the dramatic talent that enables people to mimic other voices and languages. In Montreal, city of so many languages, I have marvelled at the ease with which some people can quickly pick up an oral facility in a new language, apparently without self-consciousness, and they include Irish people I have known. I have managed a certain competence in French, but I believe I do share a post-colonial inheritance with many of my compatriots: maybe the notion that another language imposes an identity, as when an actor takes on a role, was both attractive and disturbing from the beginning. Who is the actor when he is not on stage, or is he more truly himself when he is on stage? Whose voice should I speak in? What stage should I stand on? A pervasive self-questioning about expression and sincerity, about the relativity of audiences, may well lie behind the extraordinary number of world-class dramatists who have come from the small island of Ireland.

It may have been a series of accidents beginning in that small village school that led me to Montreal, but it now seems that a mysterious logic was at work. Perhaps it is my very need to find a story in all this that arranges it this way: who can tell? It was partly my wish to be in a French city (although not wholly French), and my wish to be in North America rather than Britain (although not the United States). Such things were conscious, as was the choice of university, but in wishing to avoid European imperialisms, I would find myself living in Canada, in the bilingual city of Montreal, where French accents and English accents can be heard in all their regional and global variations, where origins and names count for so little. It would take me some time to appreciate the cultural richness of this immigrant city, experienced every day, and most of all the freedom not to be correct or authentic. And surely it is part of the mysterious logic that I would end up as a teacher of English and a writer, forever revising my sentences.

Here there is no *blas*, and yet I live with the memory of it, knowing my failure to master it in a certain way prepared me for this fluid future life. I was not converted to the idea of a sanctioned cultural identity, not in Ireland, and not in Quebec. In fact, the opposite happened: I became a kind of migrant in a shifting city. I entered on a life of change, even as the city was changing, even as it became home. While the *blas* is one other impossible ideal in life, in the dreams of cultural purists and zealots, it remains part of me to a degree. Sometimes I wish for an expression that is not compromised by the limited words available to me; that is truly mine. Perhaps it is why I am a writer. The words of another Irishman who spent his lifetime translating himself back and forth between English and French keep echoing in my head "Who is this saying it's me?"

FIVE

When I left Ireland for Montreal, I said goodbye twice, but I had persuaded myself that I wasn't really saying goodbye at all. In anticipation of my time in Quebec, *bonjour* and *au revoir* seemed more my style, light words said quickly, *farewell* a heavy word in heartfelt songs, tragedies of wartime or exile. At the age of twenty-two, who wants to face the word *farewell?* Endings seem to go against nature. I had not yet awoken to ironies at the heart of things, even in simple expressions like *au revoir*. I did not know the first truth of the oldest Greek philosopher: that we never do have the chance to see again, that change is our nature, endings and beginnings a comforting way of imagining that the flow has a shape. At Dublin Airport, I felt the inevitable weight of such natural knowledge but preferred to think that endings happened to other people.

Decades later, I keep in my mind the snapshot image of three figures on the roof of the departure lounge. Maybe they took pictures of each other and sent them to me. What I keep is what I think I remember seeing, framed by the airplane window. The image was imprinted as I tried to look away, wishing that the plane would move, looking back for the last, last glance at those waving figures that could not see me.

The figure that stood out was my girlfriend. She was in her long wet-look coat with the gold buckles that I knew so well. She wore it over a miniskirt, and her shoes were also white with gold buckles. She was dressed in a Carnaby Street style, and her hair fell long and limp like Marianne Faithful's or Twiggy's. That morning, hair and coat were blowing in the wind that swept the observation terrace.

I knew that she was deeply unhappy at my leaving. She could not believe that I would upset her so, that I would put my desire for even more studies ahead of my attention to her, to think of my own ambition rather than her feelings of loss and despair. She feared for the future, she knew about change, she was able to believe in farewell, for she had already lived through the finality of departure. It was not that she had lived through the break-up of another relationship in which her feelings had changed, or another man had left her, for he had changed. A short time before I met her, the father to whom she was irrevocably attached had died at an early age. He had been ill for a long time, he was not expected to survive, as they say, but he had survived for years beyond the predictions. He had defied death through her teenage years, his joy in living each day for the pleasures and adventures he could find was a model to her, a heroic model, for his gregarious talents and resources were ones she wished to find in herself. She admired him unconditionally, and then he died of a heart attack at the age of fifty-four. He was not her first death – there had been many that figured large in her house, and in her town – but his was the one that would give meaning to the word for the rest of her life.

The modern love affair that we had slipped into the previous winter happened in the shadow of that farewell, although, of course, we gave little thought to ghosts. It began so quickly and became so central to our lives that it seemed to escape from all the traditional games of dating, of asking out, and pacing the stages of commitment en route to engagement – the experience of her girlfriends and cousins – cautious arrangements of trade-offs behind the overwhelming desires for romance and security. I was different from the men and boys she met at her work in the insurance company or in city dancehalls, and the reality of present passion, even for honest talk and honest listening, for the adventure of experience itself, promised, I could tell, a partnership that delighted her.

After going out a few times, we were meeting every day, often for supper at Mrs. Gaj's restaurant on Lower Baggot Street, or after her evening classes or my research at the library in Trinity. We couldn't see enough of each other. She was taking night courses for her degree, and soon after we met, I left my job in the civil service and returned to University College Dublin to complete another degree. We would cross the cobbled square and have coffee or a hot whiskey somewhere around Grafton Street before heading out to Donnybrook, she to her shared bed-sitter on Morehampton Road, I to the bedroom I shared in a house on Victoria Street. Very soon we found opportunities for privacy in these places, and then the monthly panic about pregnancy raised our love affair onto the level of something like a marriage. We knew only one couple who lived as we did, it was like a love affair in a novel or a film, but the fears and the drama we kept secret. And so my decision to leave for Canada was shocking, almost a betrayal of our shared responsibility for the life we were creating together.

On either side of her on this morning were two friends. Looking back now, I can see that the intense friendships of university days create a provisional life. In my case, this illusion of a community had buoyed up a country boy in the big city so much that I could dream of lifelong friendships. I assumed that the people and places I had become attached to would stay in that eternal present of days passed around St. Stephen's Green, South Circular Road, Harold's Cross, and Rathmines. The notion of life as a state of perpetual loss and recreation might have crossed my mind in my reading of Yeats or Joyce, but what did it mean outside the heady patterns of literary and philosophical word puzzles? In my own way, I had chosen to end it all, although it would soon end anyway, as classmates settled into jobs and relationships, moved away to teach, or disappeared from view altogether.

The culmination of those years in Dublin, the desperate closeness of those friendships, the unknown future hovering over the scene: all that, I struggled to keep under control as the plane began to taxi down the runway, for I had another ordeal ahead. After a short flight across the country, we were going to touch down at Shannon where my parents would be waiting.

My father and mother had driven thirty miles from the farm to be at Shannon for this half-hour stop en route. My aging father cried, but already, on the short flight, I had collected myself and found some distance. I was aware of his tears – I expected them – and all around us, as we said our goodbyes, were sobbing parents, in some cases, wailing parents. They had come from the bar, and the loud voices and erratic actions made it seem as if they had been drowning their sorrows in an all-night party.

For a second, I felt part of the Irish diaspora, stretching back generations to the Great Famine and beyond: the finality of departure, this leaving not much different from a death in the family. The grieving could take a lifetime, if the songs were to be believed, the loss of the first home a wound that remained uncured. My mother and father grew speechless in their sober grief, spectators too at the awkward dramas of rupture – such primal terrors unleashed in the shiny surroundings outside the duty-free shop. What was there to say?

I quickly removed myself from the mythology of that mass exodus. My leaving was different. I was going to North America with all the others and the ghosts that hovered all around us, but I was only going for a short time, and I was going to Montreal, a Canadian and yet a French city. I was not leaving for work, or because I had to: I was leaving by choice, and my privileged state set me apart. I was not going to belong in the stories of exile or sink into Irish North America. Going away to graduate school was my effort to break out of my island and its self-obsessed mythologies, I said to myself, to gain some cosmopolitan experience, and then I could return as my own man. This was a different kind of myth, of life as an experiment or investment, made possible by the sixties and supported by the ease of air travel: some of this I tried to tell my parents, to reassure them that what they feared would not come to pass – that when I returned I would be a stranger.

In fact, I did feel certain that the New World would leave me untouched, for I scarcely believed in its existence. Constructed of television and magazine images, of movies like *Easy Rider* and groups like The Beach Boys and Simon and Garfunkel, of eclectic reading and condescending clichés, it was more like a dreamscape one might move through, fearful or entertained, to emerge at the other end essentially unchanged. It was hardly a departure at all. I still believed I was in control of this much of my life and that I could choose what I wanted to bring back with me when I returned.

And yet somewhere inside the wishes, the illusions and false confidence, I knew the truth — that my real life was about to begin — and in spite of everything I told myself and other people, my deepest feeling was an almost paralyzing fear of the future. Perhaps by going it was that fear I wanted to conquer.

As we rose high above the fields of County Clare and out across the coastline, soon leaving the ocean out of sight below, my very young head was more than ever full of arguments, and I knew it. The certainties that I was able to offer my girlfriend in Dublin and then my parents were words, no more than that, but for a long time now I had made my way with words, convincing words for myself first and then for the others. Scholarship boy, I had been impressing teachers for years, and then, my confidence growing with the exam results, I was encouraged to have great expectations, high ambitions. All through school I could win prizes with essays, with general knowledge contests, with public-speaking competitions, and could even win jobs at the end of it, good jobs, permanent and pensionable jobs, so what was it that drove me away from the predictable path of success in Dublin? With my job in the civil service, it had been very much within my reach, but I had left that too.

"Head in the clouds," my father had often said; "all talk'; "paper never refused ink." He had never directly questioned my decisions, but his quick dismissal of others must have included me. I could imagine him thinking this of my left-wing politics. Campaigning for the Labour Party, of all things: what would *you* know about a day's work? Hard-working farmers, from morning to night, winter and summer, had little time for workers who clocked in and out, had paid holidays and pensions. And the prime example I heard him and my uncle reassure each other with was the roads maintenance crew, the county council workers who, whenever you passed, were resting on their shovels.

Nothing was worth an argument for him, however, and so he said little, but I knew he disapproved of my political commitments and of my interest in the various revolutions of the sixties that turned up on the television news. He observed the images and shook his head. It was all "foreign," he used to say of the news, and he was not really speaking of geographical location when he used that word. How much of anything beyond the local he tried to understand or had a way of understanding I did not know, for he did not read and spoke mostly in truisms and proverbs, in a colloquial style. It was a dialect of universal certainty.

*

In 1965, the year before the commemoration of the fiftieth anniversary of the Easter Rising, numerous events were planned, including a literary competition for young people. I sent in a poem, and in all the years since, I find it more and more incredible that I was actually the winner. My effort garnered a prize of fifty pounds – a considerable sum then for a seventeen-year-old – and a handshake from President Éamon de Valera at Árus an Uachtaráin.

Equally incredible, as I look back, is what I decided to do with the money: I went to Berlin. Alone. Knowing not a word of German. I had met a young Berliner and his wife on their honeymoon in Ireland. Jürgen and Marianne had been inspired by reading the popular *Irish Journal* by Heinrich Böll, and since my mother had just listed our house as a Farm Guesthouse, they came to stay. They encouraged me to come to Berlin. Suddenly, the city became a place I could travel to, I had a safe human connection to this most dangerous and mythical of cities in contemporary news reports; this was an opportunity I had to take.

I had read *The Longest Day, Hitler's Last Days,* and other popular histories of the war, and so it may be that I had some kind of fantasy of coming close to a central historical reality of the twentieth century. By then I felt that what had happened in Germany, Central Europe, and the Normandy beaches felt of greater significance in the world than Easter 1916. Checkpoint Charlie and the Wall were the images of the city I had seen in *Time* magazine. I read everything I could find about the Iron Curtain that had closed off whole countries of Eastern Europe inside the Soviet Empire. The silence and secrecy that prevailed throughout that part of the world, as in China and Cuba, fascinated me so much that I had taken to listening to Radio Moscow broadcasts on shortwave radio. My father had told me of Lord Haw Haw's nighttime broadcasts from Nazi Germany, so that may have stirred my interest in the idea of East/West propaganda and how one might discover the truth. In a way that now bewilders me, I appear to have entertained a fantasy of crossing through the checkpoint to see things for myself on the other side of the Wall. What I thought I was going to do there amidst the ruins of the Second World War and the Cold War, what I thought I was going to discover, I cannot imagine, although Jürgen encouraged such a fantasy when he told me that he had family members on the other side whom they had not been able to contact since the Wall was built.

I had already by this time spent part of a summer in France, so this was not my first time travelling out of Ireland, although, oddly, I had never been to London or anywhere in Britain. In France I had stayed with French families and had been chaperoned around; I had never really travelled alone. In any case, with my fifty pounds in hand and perhaps a few pounds more, I made my way to Paris and on to Cologne. There I visited the cathedral, my reason for getting off the train, but what I remember is how a small incident brought home to me that I was alone and vulnerable, essentially helpless if anyone wished to attack me, and that nobody in the world knew where I was. I could disappear. I was sitting on a bench overlooking the Rhine eating a sandwich when a man sat next to me and tried to begin a conversation in German. A more secure or mature traveller would have welcomed any communication with a local in a public place, or at least would have waited, but I immediately sensed danger and concluded that he was planning some kind of aggression, maybe to steal my wallet. I panicked and rushed away, wondering if there was something about my appearance that betrayed the naivety and vulnerability I felt.

I then caught the overnight train to Berlin, to be awakened at the East German border by the loud, rough voices of guards checking documents. They carried submachine guns. I was terrified. I had never seen an armed soldier before or been interrogated in a language I did not understand. From this point on we were behind the Iron Curtain. Would I be taken away to a labour camp, never to be heard from again? Would I be allowed to travel on to Berlin?

I was, and there I made contact with Jürgen, who had found a student hostel for me to stay at. As he drove me around,

I had my first glimpse of the Wall and the Brandenburg Gate, its arches bricked up. In the evening, Jürgen took me to a bar and introduced me to German beer. At that stage, I had never even sat in an Irish pub drinking beer. Then Jürgen showed me where the ladies of the night paraded in their white dresses. It was all more than I could handle, but he did not seem to realize the depth of my inexperience and fear. He left me at a subway stop to find my way to the hostel. On the train, I was targeted by a menacing man who sat down opposite me and made some of his sexual preoccupations very clear. I was too paralyzed to move away. Again, I wondered why he had chosen me. Thinking he would not have time to follow me, at my stop, I rushed out of the carriage at the last minute and walked quickly out of the station. Suddenly, in the shadows of the wooded park near the hostel, a noise right behind me revealed his presence just as he was about to grab me. I had been a champion sprinter at school and managed to outrace him and get into the hostel safely.

Long before I came to cross over into East Berlin, day by day my terror intensified. I was alone and frequently lost and searching for someone who spoke English who might help me. I imagined that in this city, of all cities, everywhere I turned I was in danger. But how could I be in Berlin and not go behind the Wall? And I did, crossing beneath it on the subway network, the hub of which was now in the Eastern sector. Soldiers with submachine guns guarded the access to lines that left the hub for the West, to prevent any of their citizens from taking this escape route. Somehow I made my way, and soon I was on Unter den Linden, looking towards the Brandenburg Gate from the other side. I noted that a translation of *The Hostage* was playing at the State Theatre and wondered what ideological message Behan's play was supposed to teach. A few blocks from this avenue of official buildings were ruins and open spaces, still undeveloped since the levelling of the city by the Russian army twenty years before.

Suddenly a loud proclamation on a public address system spooked me – were they coming to get me? – until I realized it was the changing of the guard at the War Memorial. I happened to be sitting on a bench near the Memorial when the blaring began, and then the new soldiers goose-stepped up the street, defusing my terror a little, although the militaristic harshness of the whole ritual was designed to convey a clear message. I smelled the violence in the air, as, undoubtedly, many East German citizens had and actually experienced its coercive grip, and learned in one way or another to live with it, or to disappear, as the notorious files of the Stasi secret police would reveal after the regime collapsed and the Wall came down.

But what I remember still of these few moments sitting on the bench was an old man on the next bench, also alone. I imagined him as a prisoner of the regime. And then a young woman and a child walked towards him, and he came to life. They greeted him in high excitement, and the woman opened a cardboard box to show him what they had just bought: new shoes for his grandchild. They sat on the bench together admiring the shoes.

The intimate reality of such a moment is what travel offers, if we are able to see it, and it helped me briefly to gain perspective on the melodrama of state violence being acted out at the monument. I still remember it, but it was because it contrasted with everything else on that terrifying visit to Berlin. I was not ready to travel alone or into countries where I did not speak the language or where violence was a fact of daily life, in public and in private. Berlin intensified my fear and my sense of being alone and vulnerable, and even though I did travel elsewhere before I finally left for Canada, still hoping to get the measure of the wide world, this experience had overwhelmed me and remained an overshadowing reality for a long time.

*

A day after arriving in Montreal, I made my way to McGill University. I was not entirely alone on arrival, because there were two graduate students from Dublin with whom I'd had brief contact earlier and who were now helping me to figure out the lie of the land: the student "ghetto" next to McGill, where they had apartments, the campus, and the downtown just a stone's throw away, down the central avenue and out the Roddick Gates. I had had final exams to write in Dublin, and so I arrived late. The Director of Graduate Studies was unsure what to do with me. Teaching assignments had been given out, and my fellow graduate students in the English Department had already started meeting their freshmen classes. I had to do something to earn the money the university had guaranteed to me and so I was assigned as assistant to the professor of an upper-level course. I had unusual luck in the person I was assigned to, although, as I look back at those first years in Montreal, I am no longer sure what counts as luck, or if I should think of anything in that way. Perhaps it was that I didn't know how to take advantage of my good fortune, or to take advantage of anything, for almost everything of those years now seems shaded with anxiety and self-defeating fear. The facts of my arrival and early years, my circumstances in the city, seem to confirm my good luck, my privileged status in this high-ranking university, but that was not at all how it felt or how I interpreted my situation.

In fact, the more high-ranking I was told McGill was, the more I wondered how I had managed to be accepted, or what right I had to be there. So it had to be luck, something close to a mistake or a misunderstanding, but whenever I felt like this, I told myself that I would be going back to Dublin in a year, that I had never really expected to survive in a North American graduate school in the first place. At university in Dublin, I had been inspired by an Englishman who had taught in Toronto for four years. There were other inspiring teachers also, many of them, but as I worked my way through my degree, he said to me, "Get out!" He encouraged me to apply to Canadian universities for scholarships. This appealed to me because there was no question of going to the US during the Vietnam years, and funding for further studies in Ireland or the UK was scarce. When I had a few offers, he said, "Go to Montreal!" And so I did, to McGill, living off his confidence in me although I had never taught, or marked undergraduate essays, or done research for a professor, the kind of work he told me I would be paid to do. He knew I could do it, and so I had to believe him.

The Director eventually told me that I would assist Professor Blaise, who had a very large class for her course, "Great Writings of Europe, 1850-1950." Her name sounded French, and so, much focused on the French I had heard around me at the airport the day before, and making my way downtown, I assumed, naturally enough, that I would be meeting and working with someone from Montreal. Perhaps we would even speak French, something that would really enrich my time here and help me to integrate into the life of the city. I made my way upstairs to the third floor of the Arts Building, the oldest on the campus, and knocked on a heavy, oak door.

The person who greeted me was dressed in a sari and wore many gold bracelets. I was stunned. She was Indian, young, and strikingly beautiful, and she was smiling in welcome. She spoke in an accent I had never heard, certainly not Indian, I decided quickly, as if I could really know, but it seemed somewhere between British and American, precise and articulate but with a colloquial or conversational rhythm. She was friendly, poised and refined, a touch aristocratic perhaps, and as I tried to absorb all this and the colourful posters of Hindu festivals (I assumed) on the walls, she sat me down and told me about her course. I was far out of my depth already, mesmerized, seduced by the fluent intellectual energy, the ease and articulacy of her delivery. The reading list for her course spoke of so much literature already appreciated, digested, lectured on, and her personal aura of cosmopolitan culture came out of a larger world than anything I had encountered in Dublin. Denis Donoghue, professor of modern English and American literature, was my only reference point, for he seemed to float in a mid-Atlantic accent somewhere beyond the borders of an Irish place or culture.

Professor Blaise told me she had already given some introductory lectures on European philosophy and the rise of modernism. Then she had started her lectures on *The Portrait of a Lady*, so I would need to catch up on that, but since I had come from Dublin, she was confident I would be able for all this – there would even be Joyce's *A Portrait* later. The students were reading *Swann's Way* for next week; after that it would be Mann's *Death in Venice*, Gide's *The Immoralist,* and later there would be some Lawrence, Camus, Sartre, and Beckett, not to forget Forster's *A Passage to India*. I tried to stay calm until I left the office, my mind spinning at the list of books I had never read and knew next to nothing about. University College Dublin had not prepared me for this. There was never any European literature in translation on our courses. How could I possibly be of some use to the seminar groups I would meet each week for discussion of the books and any matter that came up in Professor Blaise's lectures? It would take me all week to prepare for each seminar, to have anything at all to say, and so how would I find time to do any work in my own program, or mark the exams and papers that would be coming in during the year, about ninety each time.

A new professor, Bharati Blaise had a reputation already for being brilliant, and other graduate students told me they had fled from her seminar on symbolism. My students were intimidated and awe-struck. She breezed through these classic works, dropping names like Schopenhauer, Nietzsche, and Bergson: they admired her and they hated her; few understood what she was saying. She was a goddess of the academy, truly a person of another class or species, on a pedestal, so beautiful as to frighten many of her students and, I came to think, her colleagues also. I too was frightened by the challenge she offered me in my teaching and in the marking. And yet she set a standard. The academic world and the world of literature had suddenly moved ahead of me, but with her guiding spirit, I wanted to catch up. I wanted to be inspired by her. I wanted to impress her.

Out of my depth, I was tense and adrift, and the student parties added to my tension. I felt naïve and gauche, again a country boy in a big city, as I had felt in Dublin. Everyone seemed to have a style of being in the world, at ease chatting, and chatting each other up. This was still the sixties in spirit, and I had never worn blue jeans, never smoked dope or dropped acid, and was very faithful to my girlfriend back in Dublin. Everyone else was surely liberated into an experimental social life, which was, after all, the only authentic life. I had always been the youngest in my class, all through schooldays and during my Dublin years; the feeling that everyone else was older and more experienced, more sure of themselves, followed me to Montreal and contributed to the sense that it was only others who could take initiative, not I. I had joined the sixties revolution in Dublin, took part in all the street demonstrations, and now I realized that in North America, in addition to anti-Vietnam and social justice, the revolution was about lifestyle, especially about sex, and I was still trapped in my insular, puritanical, upbringing.

Panic and stress permeated my days. I assumed that I was doing a bad job while wanting so much to do a good one, forever feeling unprepared, and behind, but I was a poor judge of my own performance. The facts of my accomplishments so far should have underwritten a good measure of self-confidence, but the bursts of impassioned self-assertion that allowed for these accomplishments masked a deeper and lasting anxiety. Ambition and discipline were often resting on a shifting foundation of insecurity, of shame, of anger, of bewilderment. I was twenty-two, but I was still a child, easily embarrassed or caught off guard, my pink skin blushing to a high red, words failing me.

★

I met Iztok some months later at Vanier College. He had studied at the University of Toronto and so was not one of my fellow-students at McGill who had applied en masse. He and I were offered jobs, and so we were brought together one day because we were going to be colleagues. He invited me to his apartment for supper, poured me a glass of slivovitz, and began to prepare schnitzel. I had never eaten veal or heard of this drink. I had never met anyone for whom cooking was such a sacred ritual. The delicacy of his attention, the awe of his commentary, the precision of his method enchanted and intimidated me. Then he started to open other bottles; after Pinot Grigio and Tokaj, I stopped remembering names, for my appreciation of each new taste was overwhelmed by the ambience he had created. Iztok's enthusiasms in food, wine, books, and movies were voiced against a background of jazz; the music was foreign to me too, all saxophone solos and intimate women's voices breaking with loneliness and heartbreak.

He had lived a lifetime already, it seemed, or else he had absorbed lifetimes of sensual knowledge and then the world-weariness that made my striving for understanding just so juvenile. Taste and style, not understanding, were what mattered. He had been writing a dissertation on modern American poetry. When he mentioned names like Frank O'Hara and Kenneth Patchen, I was lost and felt insular, stuck with my English and Irish names, and when his real enthusiasms came out and he quoted lines from "Spring in Fialta" and *Pnin* and spoke of Nabokov as the only arbiter of taste, I was utterly lost. The world was suddenly revolving, not just around a centre in Canada or America, but around a Europe beyond the English language, and beyond French literature, towards a Slavic and Russian world that had never really been translated for me – this was not only the somewhat nostalgic world of Chekhov and Gogol, but of Communism, war, disappearances and iron borders.

While American jazz and baseball had been the textures of Iztok's teenage years, and he affected an American cool in his sixties (or was it fifties?) hipster pose, deeper springs could be felt when he spoke of Nabokov, the displaced European gentleman, living now in Switzerland after the commercial and aesthetic success of *Lolita*, far from the vulgarity and stupidity of the American life he had been exiled in. Nabokov's hauteur was an image of pure style, above and beyond the bloody revolutions and mass slaughters that had been European history in his lifetime. There were fools everywhere the only defence an absolute certainty of taste, an erudition (about butterflies and other things, especially languages), and a stinging wit that left the opposition reeling in uncertainty. In asides, Iztok spoke of hotels and trains as his favourite places, which I understood to mean that expatriation must be embraced as an art, but it was only as the years went by that I realized how much he had made Nabokov his mentor in the art of living.

He wrote articles for a Canadian magazine under the name A. D. Person, and often used the expression "a D.P." As Tito consolidated his power in Yugoslavia, Iztok's father had to flee Slovenia and had come to Canada a few years ahead of his wife and two children. They had remained behind, just avoiding the Displaced Persons camp in Germany. I had never heard of this expression or these camps, or known much of the lives that had disappeared in the other camps, or of the survivors. And soon I knew that the lives of many people in Canada had been similarly shaped by one war or another, their exile, their settling, their feelings about returning.

Iztok's own way of going back was in words, and especially in translation. The poet he translated, Kocbek, did not leave, did not have to leave, for he had been an active anti-fascist, lending support to Tito's Communist-led partisans, and becoming, briefly, a government minister, but during the thirty years of life that remained, he was silenced by Tito and spied on by no less than sixty-nine informants, his life possibly spared by his literary eminence. He did not write overtly dissident or confrontational poetry, and in Iztok's introduction, he says that "the only Kocbek worth bringing into English" is the "small, local poet" who writes "country music." At least, this was Iztok's preference in a large body of work, and his favourite poem gave the volume its title *Na Vraith Zvecer / At the Door at Evening*:

> A mother to her daughter at evening
> as she is setting out
> all beautiful and clean
> a mother to her daughter at the door
> that she might stop her
> a mother to her daughter at the door at evening
> that she might stop her and tell her
> tell her the communication from antiquity today derided
> and already her throat constricts and she can't manage the sentence
> can't manage the one redeeming sentence
> as no mother has ever managed
> no mother ever to her daughter at the door at evening
> to her daughter and her lineage
> for the daughter will return
> she will return changed
> she will return with her own fruit
> one day she too will feel her throat constrict
> as will her daughter and her daughter's daughter
> at the door at evening

In later years, Iztok's period of writing these loving translations over, he went on to write mocking, exiled, and ironic columns for a Slovenian newspaper, letters from North America, letters from the time when his parents realized they would not go back, and neither would he.

Meeting Iztok so soon after my arrival began my education in migration. So many of the people I eventually came to know had fled to Canada from history. Growing up on my island, I had known little about any history other than the Irish and the English, the Catholics and the Protestants. It had been codified for us in school and in popular mythology: a simple case of conquerors and conquered, new chapters of the same story over and over, down through six or seven centuries. In the end, history was a simple story, the same teams always battling over the same piece of ground. There was a kind of shame attached to invisibility; those who were not part of the national story had in some way betrayed the nation or were second-class citizens. The more complex histories of those who absented themselves from the scene, or did not figure in the battles, were unknown to us. Emigrants, with few exceptions, had chosen invisibility, and insofar as those who stayed at home gave the matter any thought, it was to assume that they only ever wished to return and that the better life they hoped for was not attainable.

Ever since the Famine – an event that was undoubtedly part of history – Irish emigrants to Britain, North America, and Australia could with justice be portrayed as victims, casualties of economic and political exploitation, who were suffering too in their exiled condition, although, of course, I grew up in a country that had been separate from the British Empire for more than a generation. For many it remained true that they felt like exiles, inheritors of a common fate, sheltered in their loss by belonging to an aggrieved community. But to think of them in their new place, as separate individuals performing the difficult dance with present time, shaping themselves as they were shaped by the new circumstances, creating a new generation in a new place: that was beyond our imaginations or the imaginations of those who invented our local versions of history for us.

And yet without my even thinking of it, this was an outline of my story, not of exile and the tragic history of Ireland, as I had been trained to think, but of migration and settling in a new place. To a degree, it is the story of every adult who moves outside his home parish, the invention of an adult life at a tangent to received mythologies of identity and place and history, yet it is only in recent decades that the freedom to do so without going far away from the expectations and judgments of home has been possible. When I took that direct flight from Shannon to Montreal, I did not realize that between the leaving and the arrival, gulfs of space and time would open – here and there, then and now – and much less visible or even imaginable, an abyss of doubt, a desperate sense that whatever talent I might have had was useless in this new place, that – in spite of what Bharati Blaise and others tried to tell me – in some way I had lost my talent or did not yet know how to manage it.

*

I was too young to recognize or understand much of the anxiety that gripped me as I left for Montreal, the fear, the terror even, of a disappearing self. Out of my place, who was I?

If I knew nobody, and nobody knew me, who would I be? How would anyone in this new place, this different place, interpret me? Such questions are an exaggeration, of course, for nothing real is conducted on such a level of abstraction, but fears of dislocation are reflected in them, the fear that there is a space beyond familiar markers where signposts are unreadable and people unfathomably strange. Or so one tells oneself, finding the evidence there to confirm alienation rather than discovering what might be familiar or constant in other cultures and places.

It is, of course, why chain migration is the most comfortable way to leave, to join a family member or someone known or trustworthy already settled, as so many Irish did in coming to North American cities, there to be integrated into a transplanted community that spoke the dialect of the tribe. In such circumstances, my questions would not have arisen; one might allow oneself to be recognized as "one of us," one's attitudes and goals taken for granted, one's freedom to be different sacrificed for the balm of security and belonging. Integration in the new place follows rules that are not much different from what they are in one's original place.

But for a long time already I had felt different, an awkward outsider in every gathering, except for a time with a few friends in Dublin, and this new test was actually no different from the tests I had always felt I was undergoing in Ireland. In this sense, my whole upbringing may have been a preparation for this day. Irish nationalism, its histories and its mythologies, its signs and symbols, its orthodoxies and its exclusions, had been an enveloping belief, almost as powerful and holistic as a religion, and in addition there was an actual Church that was certainly holistic and exclusive, the policing of its doctrines and practices even more intimately coercive. Although my parents were not fanatically doctrinal or devotional, I grew up a pious boy, a literalist of belief, certain in my reliance on the intimate presence of a personal God, accepting of a cosmic theological order, and scrupulously unquestioning in all the finer points of what priests and teachers told us. Perhaps it was the collapse of all this that had left me fearful of the absence of a cosmic or local order, unforgivingly demanding of others' behaviour, and most especially of my own. I may have been my own enemy, forever examining my conscience. Perhaps it was my secret adolescent struggle with this inheritance that triggered my fear of going even further into isolation in my own head, constantly aware that my experiment in living had left me uncertain of everything; perhaps I was suffering from the loss of the very thing I had set myself against.

If I were of a calmer disposition, I would know that in Montreal things would take place one event at a time, one day at a time, one personal encounter at a time, as always, but back then my epic notions of myself, my confidence and my doubt, my hauteur, my shame and embarrassment, my knowledge and my ignorance were all intertwined. The crash of self-esteem or the summoning of poise happened almost by accident. I had little sense of why I was overwhelmed by one or the other. But I knew already that I was many selves, or many growing selves, or potential selves, never sure which one would let me down or buoy me up in new circumstances, never sure which ones would assist me in becoming the authentic person I aspired to be. Confident, clear-headed, articulate, how was it that I could slide so quickly into an awkward, embarrassed, tongue-tied state? So often decisive, I could sink into a mood of procrastination.

Why did I not instinctively know who I was and get on with relating to people without the stress that had me sweating and weak, heading towards a panic attack?

And now I had pushed myself to the limit. What was I going to be as a temporary sojourner? An expatriate, a landed immigrant (my official status in Canada), or simply an emigrant, but none of these words carried any meaning for me yet.

*

The undercurrents of confusion would not leave me even as I became a graduate student at McGill, and then a full-time college teacher, or when I married and my first son was born, or when I became a Canadian citizen five years later. An unnamed anxiety remained at the heart of me, an anxiety about failure or loss or shame or guilt, even when the accomplishment that would free me from such feelings was really unclear. In spite of all the evidence of my good luck, my success, the love and respect of my parents, my wife and son and colleagues, something did not feel right in the limbo state I could too easily slip into.

For a very long time, deep down, I would continue to feel at sea, anxious and uncertain, and it was the love of my wife and my children that helped me through these years, but I did not yet say goodbye, or, I mean, a final goodbye, for I said many goodbyes along the way. The focus of my anxiety, often expressed as anger, was McGill University, for I had never found my place there, and it may be that the standards set for me by Bharati Blaise in all things to do with the university alienated me, for it gradually emerged that she was alienated too. But I do not really think it was my admiration for her, since I had come to McGill with very high expectations following my years in University College Dublin. My absence from McGill when I began to teach full-time took on a life of its own. I had shown that I did not really make graduate school my priority, something that my professors there may have felt as a slight or simply a sign that I was disinterested; at any rate, I soon began to feel that I was an outsider there and I had not really been given a place. I had done little to deserve a place, of course, and so I began to feel ashamed of my impotence in failing to move decisively towards completing my doctorate. It was respect I craved, but at McGill I didn't find many people whose respect I valued. Most likely it was the respect of my former teachers back in Ireland I craved. Perhaps my confusion, disillusionment, and anger were due to the fact that I had idealized the university and higher education, had found a new Church, made my teachers into priests of the new faith. At McGill I encountered attitudes of such pragmatism and professional ambition that I thought literature and literary studies were demeaned, my faith dismissed as sentimentality about art. Years began to slip by, and my sense of failure grew; yet I stubbornly refused to withdraw from the doctoral program. After all, this was why I had come to Canada in the first place; I must endure.

I had to give up all hope of ever finding a job in Ireland: at the back of my mind, for some time, I had wanted to return to a university teaching position, but how could I go back now? I felt trapped and, whatever I thought of my fate, I knew I was here to stay. The girlfriend I had left behind had become my wife and had joined me in Montreal, also thinking that our stay would be limited. She had always wanted to return to be close to her family, and so my failure to find a way to return trapped her.

Once or twice I interviewed for an academic position, but I concluded sourly that the positions were allocated on the basis of connections rather than merit. I had little claim to merit anything back in Ireland, however, even if the job I had, the scholarships I had won, my few publications might add up to something in Canada, but overall my failure to finish enveloped me. My wife went to graduate school also during these years and eventually won a teaching position at another college, a position she would never have been able to achieve in Ireland. Our two salaries would eventually enable us to buy the old house close to McGill.

More important than respect, of course, is love, and what is lucky about those years is that my wife stayed with me and offered what support she could. A more pragmatic person than I, she was very happy with the opportunity Canada had opened up for her, and she became a much-admired and loved teacher. Without her love for me during these years of drifting, I might have perished in the McGill ghetto.

One day as I passed by the Classics bookstore in Les Terraces, the newly opened shopping centre downtown, I paused to look in the clearance bin by the door. The Penguin edition of V. S. Naipaul's *In a Free State* caught my attention, no doubt because at many levels the title seemed to speak to me. I still have it, along with every book that Naipaul has written. The style of the book, its voices and depth of emotion, and its blending of fiction and travel journal extracts caught me off guard, yet in some way, its generic fluidity converted me to possibilities of writing that I had paid little attention to up until then.

Naipaul freed me to think of prose as an exploratory and intimate medium, and even if he called *The Enigma of Arrival* and *A Way in the World* novels, I did not believe him, and these books, and especially *Finding the Centre*, gave me a way of thinking about the world and about writing that made me an uncritical reader of his work and would later, I have no doubt, become part of the role as writer I set for myself. The many versions of leaving Trinidad as a young scholar en route to Oxford and then anchoring himself in England, becoming a writer and discovering how to return to his origins were all hypnotizing. But it was not exactly that Naipaul's theme was my theme, his experience a key to mine; it was his way with language and observation, his way of reflecting an understanding of himself and his life that went deeper than ideas into a state of sublime knowledge.

SIX

It is evident to me now that teachers were always surrogate fathers, English teachers in particular, beginning with my teacher in the village who acted Christy Mahon in *The Playboy* and then my English teacher in the monastery school.

Gus was a young teacher, small with fair hair that curved back from his forehead in two long waves. He liked to read to us, and as he chanted the poem, the words took on an aura of special meaning and power, almost like the Latin of the monks. "The trees are in their autumn beauty, / The woodland paths are dry, / Under the October twilight the water / Mirrors a still sky; / Upon the brimming water among the stones / Are nine-and-fifty swans." I was transported back to the farm and the lake. I was Yeats or felt that I could be, that I too had been in such beautiful places, and I knew that Coole Park was not far from the farm across the mountains. It was the teacher's personality that gave depth to the words on the page. Mr. Martin was not acting; it was as if he had an appreciation of the inner meaning of the poem and his reading was electrified by this. He liked to fill the billiard room with his voice. It was his stage, but the class was on the stage with him.

Unlike other teachers, he made us feel that he enjoyed being with us. He invited us to enjoy with him the pleasure of literary language. That pleasure included all the work of his class. He encouraged us to write, and he praised our efforts.

He spoke of the fresh and original turns of phrase of other writers. He pulled examples out of the air, Patrick Kavanagh's description of crows over a potato field as newspapers blowing in the wind, and broke into quotation easily: "Two roads diverged in a yellow wood, / And sorry I could not travel both / And be one traveler, long I stood / And looked down one as far as I could / To where it bent in the undergrowth." His overflowing memory was a tribute to how much meaning and delight he had found in literature. Language was a storehouse of wisdom and inspiration, and in it could be found perfect ways of saying things.

We could tell that Gus Martin's years of schooling in this college and his years in university had left him rich in self-confidence. He was not simply a teacher doing his job; he allowed us to imagine him as a person much larger than the role or the subject being taught. He spoke of his own discovery of learning and of his years as a debater in University College Dublin, and we knew that confidence in personality was linked to the free way he expressed his own insights and opinions. We experienced the play of ideas, the persuasive power of words, the hypnotic charm of a man so clearly at ease with himself. We read *Animal Farm*, a novel not on the required syllabus, and as we debated the political meanings of the fable, his commentary would range widely over politics and history but would always return to the writer and his craft. Learning with Gus was an enlargement of ourselves. Knowledge was the way to self-confidence.

Gus Martin became my hero. I looked up to him because here, close to me, was an example of what might be possible in this college and in the larger world. I could win praise and appreciation for speaking up in class or for my essays. I found I had a talent for feeling what I thought Gus felt when he read. In the study hall at night I would recite and memorize the poems. I felt their rhythms because of the intensity with which I listened to the prayers in the chapel: "Tower of ivory, House of gold, Gate of heaven, Morning star." The chant to the Blessed Virgin Mary went on but, more perfectly than the prayers, the rhythm of the poem seemed mesmerizing. My yearning for perfection was real, for it had been captured in words by someone else, and this was the value of poetry.

An unusual thing happened, for at the end of my years in secondary school when I began to study at University College Dublin, Gus also moved there to become a lecturer in the English department. At first, I was excited, and his presence made me feel a little at home, but there was a disappointment, for it soon became clear to me that he would not be available to me as an advisor or mentor. He was too busy, I told myself, for whenever I went to his office, hoping to have some time with him, there were always students lined up. I waited awkwardly until the end, but by then he was rushing to get somewhere. I tried to understand: he had just moved with his family, including young children, to set up house in the city; in addition to his job at the university, he had become a presenter for schools television, and soon became the best-known English teacher in the country. He went on to set up an organization for teachers of English and to design a new curriculum for secondary schools. I realized what a dull burden I must be for such an active person, how he must hate to see me waiting, for he must have known the weight of my needy personality from before. I would have to help myself.

But something else was happening, for soon, because I had lectures from a wide range of brilliant people, I began to think of Gus's world as the secondary schools'. What earlier had been so valuable to me, his enthusiasm for literature, and especially Irish writing, now had a popularizing ring to it, his lectures depending more on his enthusiastic and appreciative manner than on original scholarship. As I got to know other English students, we did the usual thing — talked about our lecturers and compared them — and we were unforgiving. We had the highest intellectual expectations, and Gus's ideas seemed to depend on the books he mentioned as references. We had a new standard of measurement when we listened to other lecturers, yet he was the favourite lecturer of many students. He was popular with some students, but we knew they were the students who thought of the exams first, who wanted to understand him easily and write down what he said, who did not find his ideas challenging or overwhelming. And so this division into camps, according to the kind of lecturer one favoured, became a measure of ambition at this new level of intellectual development.

More was involved than snobbery, or, indeed, real differences of intellectual ability, for one's self-image as a literary type was in question. We were members of the English Literature Society, and a friend and I began to work for *St. Stephen's*, the college literary magazine. Like Stephen Dedalus in his university years, my friends and I were conscious of a community of cosmopolitan literary figures whom we wanted to believe were our peers and models. We wanted to set ourselves apart from those students who thought of themselves as secondary schoolteachers in the making; in fact, our high ambitions and standards had to do with rebellion, with emancipating ourselves from the clerical ethos of schools and education. We did not want to preserve unquestioned the provincial Catholicism of our formation and then reproduce it for another generation.

*

Some time in 1967 or 1968, Conor Cruise O'Brien became an icon in my fantasy homeland of international intellectuals and left-wing activism. He had all the right ideas for that time before the Troubles, before Ireland joined Europe – at least for me he did, in those days of the student occupation at Earlsfort Terrace, anti-Vietnam rallies outside the American Embassy, the great anti-apartheid march from O'Connell Bridge to Lansdowne Road (with O'Brien at its head), and the Civil Rights Movement in Northern Ireland.

It may be that I had read his revisionist essay on the Easter Rising when it first appeared in the *Irish Times*, and his investigation in "Passion and Cunning" of Yeats's fascist leanings was certainly talked about in literary circles. But it was the *New York Review of Books* that really introduced me to the O'Brien I needed, and it was the atmosphere in which that discovery was made that I now think significant, for in those days it was impossible to find the *New York Review*, or any such periodical, in Dublin bookshops or libraries.

In 1966, Denis Donoghue had returned from his Cambridge and American sojourns to become Professor of Modern English and American Literature. In place of the heavy weather of Leavisite solemnities, he threaded metaphysical *aperçus* through a fine web of references to philosopher-critics we had never heard of – Susanne Langer, Kenneth Burke, John Crowe

Ransom, and a host of others. Not only did he acknowledge that American Literature existed, a radical gesture in those days; he tossed about the names of current American writers and critics as if he knew them personally. Donoghue was a giant of some sort in a department previously populated by pygmies; it now seems odd, in the context of the sixties and of his later critical writing, that for us students of English, his arrival felt like a radical upheaval.

Donoghue hired many new teachers, among them Jim Mays, an Oxford graduate who had spent a number of years at the University of Toronto. It was at the Mays's house that I began to read the *New York Review* and was mesmerized, so much so that I ended up writing a thesis on Noam Chomsky, first encountered in those pages denouncing the crimes of America and the collusion of academics in the Vietnam enterprise. Why I wrote about Chomsky and not O'Brien I cannot recall – probably the influence of Mays; yet it was O'Brien's presence in the *New York Review* that had the more profound effect. And I realized that although he, like Donoghue, was an Irishman who moved in such circles, their casts of mind were very different.

Unlike Donoghue, O'Brien was down on the streets with the students, protesting about the Vietnam War and lending support to the student revolution. That is where I wanted to be. The Students for Democratic Action, a clone of the American and the French movements of 1968, organized an occupation of the administrative offices in Earlsfort Terrace, and I was there. The leaders I remember, John Feeney and Kevin Myers, had the aura of global revolution about them, Liberation Theology in Feeney's case, but it is now clear to me that what I really needed was a channel for disaffected adolescent energy

— for disappointment, anger, shame, and self-hatred. All these people contributed to mapping the channel I needed, a sense of a world elsewhere, but O'Brien was my main inspiration.

In the *New York Review*, he took on Irish, African, and American subjects with erudition and wit. It was the clarity and confidence of his voice that was liberating. During those later years of his stay as Albert Schweitzer Professor at New York University, he became a kind of intellectual father, a dissenting Irishman who had not been consumed and neutralized by timidity. Here was someone whose intellect I could trust and whose actions I could respect, and so I was ready for adoption. Fearless, he was my opposite; maybe I could find the secret and become a little like him.

"The intellectual in a priest-led community," he had written in *Writers and Politics*, "must develop strengthened means of defending himself. He acquires in the process special capabilities and special limitations, different from those affecting intellectuals in Protestant/agnostic countries. He is likely to set great store by irony, the versatile, durable and easily camouflaged weapon of every ideological guerrilla; he will take an almost morbid interest in hypocrisy." Such insight into what I felt I needed to become, such a reading of my inner need, led me to search for everything that O'Brien had written, and to turn up at Liberty Hall when he returned to Dublin to announce his candidacy for Labour in the next general election. It was then that I joined the Labour Party, although I would work on the election campaign of Dr. Noel Browne, my local candidate in Dublin South-East, rather than become a foot soldier for O'Brien.

★

I had first heard of China in the *Far East* and other missionary magazines to which my mother subscribed. At the end of the rosary each night, we prayed for "the conversion of Russia," and then, as stories were published of the brutal persecution of Irish missionaries in Mao's China, it too became a place of martyrs for the Faith. On our map of the world, Russia and China were no more real than Heaven and Hell, Purgatory and Limbo; they were visionary theatres in which the melodrama of Catholicism was acted out. Life on earth – in Russia, in China, or in Ireland – was about the hereafter, not the here and now.

When I first heard of the Cultural Revolution and Mao's *Little Red Book*, I was already spending much of my time marching and putting up posters. Moving outside the university, I entered a circle of people with overlapping left-wing affiliations. In October 1968, a few of us hitched to Belfast to take part in the big march on the Guildhall. We got there late but joined the crowd sitting down on the street, and then adjourned to the Queen's University campus for a discussion that lasted into the night and led to the founding of the People's Democracy movement. It was said that Michael Farrell and other PD leaders were Trotskyites.

Along with other young members of the Labour Party, I began to hang out at Mrs. Gaj's restaurant. Her two teenaged sons were in the Maoist grouping, the Internationalists, headquartered at Trinity, and her connections to radical activists of various stripes were well known. In January 1969, our circle joined the protest on the streets that had grown up around the imprisonment of the housing activist Denis Dennehy. We heard that he was a member of the Communist Party. We welcomed the police charge breaking up our sit-down on

O'Connell Bridge. It proved to our satisfaction that justice was on our side rather than on theirs.

Our circle knew that however radical we were, we could never be radical enough for the Internationalists, believers in Marxist-Leninism-Mao-Tse-Tung-Thought, whose version of the revolutionary truth came from the *Little Red Book*. They didn't march with the rest of us; they created their own confrontations with the police and, though a small band, succeeded in attracting much publicity. They believed in the cleansing of society of all counter-revolutionary class interests, and believed that the Cultural Revolution was necessary to preserve the purity of Mao's proletarian revolution. Mao was sometimes a poet: "all reactionaries are paper tigers." It was very easy in those days to believe that phrases like "wars of national liberation" had a true and simple meaning and were actually going to lead to something that would not be a murderous dictatorship. Such uncompromising, visionary conviction was seductive, but I didn't rush to join the Internationalists. I drew back from the bluntness of "Politics is war without bloodshed while war is politics with bloodshed."

My unfocused fervour was really a replacement for my Catholic faith and was much coloured by it. Commitment was a very serious matter and of such profound belief that the obvious could remain unseen. That's what allowed me to ignore the bloody iron of Mao's parenthesis in a rather banal statement such as "every kind of thinking, without exception, is stamped with the brand of a class." Excitement and danger were seductive for young people like me, as was the ease of self-transcendence in a Great Cause. Even the warning sign of fear could be enveloped in idealistic fantasies of a new kind of power. I had been trained to believe in absolutes and in martyrdom as the direct way to heaven. I could have been one of those students in the Cultural Revolution who moved through cities in mobs humiliating or assaulting members of their parents' generation. Closer to home, I could almost have been in the IRA, for in our talk, republicanism, socialism, and revolution were often indistinguishable notions. In all the activities of that year, I made common cause with the different left-wing groupings that were inclined to embrace all revolutionary stirrings as the real thing. Mao's mantras pervaded the atmosphere, even if within each group hairs were often split on the correct ideological line.

In fact, I was deeply confused and fearful, lost in the discussions and in the effort to clarify what it was I believed. Sitting in the library reading Herbert Marcuse and the *New Left Review* did not really help to give me absolute faith. Others seemed to have no such difficulty, and their certainty and passion were things I could share in the heat of the moment, only to have unease grip me later, along with a sense of guilt that I lacked such certainty. It seemed to me that Mao was right: my hesitation, my inability to think straight, was a symptom that revealed I was not of the right social class. Now I know it was a season in my life, and having lost one faith, it was possible to lose another; but a sense of common purpose, a provisional community, is not abandoned easily. When I left for Montreal, it was a great release.

*

Bharati Mukherjee – Blaise was her married name – appreciated my teaching and my marking, but so far had my confidence tumbled, so tongue-tied was I in her presence, that I failed to read the signs. She invited me to her house to meet Bernard Malamud, whom she knew through her husband, Clark, and whose stories and novels she greatly admired, and she also asked me to take her place at the large lecture when the class began to study Joyce. But as the year went on, and I was encouraged by other graduate students to apply for a full-time teaching position at Vanier, a new college, she wrote an excellent reference which won me an interview, and I was offered the job.

I lost touch with her, although, in truth, I remained so in awe of her that I never relaxed in her presence. It was not long until her real talent became public: her first novel, *The Tiger's Daughter*, won great praise, and it was followed by another, *Wife*, and soon she was on leave from McGill and spent two years in India. I met her by chance when she returned, and she tried to help me to get though my dissertation, but she also confessed her unhappiness at McGill and the city, and soon she was gone.

Over the years, I followed her progress in Toronto and in various places in the United States as new novels and volumes of stories came out. She revealed that her unhappiness was a consequence of the prejudice she felt as a "visible minority," and she criticized the Canadian idea of multiculturalism. In the sixties, Pierre Elliott Trudeau and others had outlined a vision of Canada as a country where new immigrants might preserve as much of their ethnic identity as possible within the broader framework of the English and French traditions of the federal system. In contrast, she favoured the American "melting-pot" approach in which all immigrants are encouraged to blend into the mainstream culture. One of her books, *Darkness and Other Stories*, I used in a course I taught on immigrant literature, and I knew that her progress as a novelist was linked to her increasing prominence as a writer about immigration: she associated herself with Jewish immigrant writers like Malamud, and cast off the sari in favour of American-style dress. She did not want to be known as Indian; she wanted to be, simply, American.

Years later, I read a talk Mukherjee gave at the New York Public Library entitled "Imagining Homelands." She explored four distinct kinds of migration: expatriation, exile, immigration, and repatriation. I discovered that at the time I knew her, she now believed she had been in the stage of expatriation, "an act of sustained self-removal from one's native culture, balanced by a conscious resistance to total inclusion in the new host society." Clearly, she felt that she moved on from this state, had to move on, even though she found it an "attractive bargain": "It is possible, in expatriation, to step out of the constraints into which one has been born and to exercise to the fullest the dual vision of the detached outsider." So many of the great "self-made" artists of the twentieth century can be seen in this way – Conrad, Beckett, Nabokov, Henry James, T. S. Eliot, V. S. Naipaul; her list goes on, and yet she did not find this stance suited her needs.

In contrast, exile is painful: "the comparative luxury of self-removal is replaced by harsh compulsion. The spectrum of choice is gravely narrowed; the alternatives may be no more subtle than death, imprisonment, or a one-way ticket to oblivion." It now appears that it was her experience in Montreal that made her feel that she was more exile in Canada than expatriate: "If expatriation is the route of cool detachment, exile is for some that of furious engagement." As I read Mukherjee's talk, I found myself thinking back to my own years at McGill, when she was there: was I an expatriate or an exile? And I had to reply an expatriate. But when I thought of Iztok, I was not sure: his cool detachment (and this was my sense of how he presented himself, gentleman jazzman) seemed to mask the furious engagement of the exile. Mukherjee went on to speak of immigration, the condition she espoused with a passion: "I am an integrationist and, to use a dirty word, a mongrelizer." She has an American/Canadian husband, her two children were born in the United States, and she has settled for the "meltingpot." The stories I liked so much in *Darkness* are stories that map these ambiguous spaces of commitment and alienation, of belonging and detachment, of interpreting how one is at home in a new place.

I was not able to interpret where I was when I was so lucky to be inspired by Bharati Mukherjee in those McGill days, both of us expatriates at that stage, although, of course, I placed her on a pedestal, and could not see how she might mirror, or not, my own condition. And while I could be more comfortable with designations, Irish, or Irish-Canadian, or Canadian, as the years went by, I did not have to experience overt racism on the streets of Montreal; with my Canadian children growing up and through adolescence, and trying to locate themselves, I began to realize that I was rooted here and there, rooted in different ways, and for my Canadian children at home in Montreal. Belonging in the French community of Quebec was another matter, how to feel at home if one is not a *vrai Québécois*, but Bharati Mukherjee had not even begun to reflect on that.

SEVEN

I came to the French-speaking city of Montreal to study at McGill, an English university situated in the "Golden Square Mile" of Anglo-Scottish wealth when the city was an outpost of the British empire. Much had changed since McGill was founded; in 1867, Confederation established a federal government structure, and, most notably, Lower Canada became Quebec. Yet there was always a minority of French descent who contested their inclusion in a balanced political structure, and beginning in the sixties, a small secret organization began a bombing campaign to assert the province's right to independence.

A fortnight after I arrived, the "October Crisis" began just a few blocks away from the university. The British Trade Commissioner was kidnapped and held hostage for six weeks by members of the *Front de Libération du Québec*. Their manifesto demanding the separation of Quebec from the rest of Canada was broadcast; the army patrolled the streets and many nationalist *sympathisants* were detained; another FLQ cell kidnapped a government minister and murdered him. Pierre Elliott Trudeau invoked the War Measures Act and declared a state of emergency. For my first two months or so, I was in a war zone.

The extraordinary thing is that I do not have a single memory of these cataclysmic events happening or of how I responded to them. The nature of Canada as a peaceful, federal country was unraveling just as I arrived, and I hardly paid attention.

I think an explanation for my amnesia is that I had come from Ireland, where the savagery of the Troubles was so intensely present in the media that this smaller-scale savagery was hardly worth my attention. Or it may be that I thought I understood the language in which the FLQ framed its thinking, its version of nationalism, that in some way the Québécois were like the Catholic Irish, and that the FLQ was similar to the IRA. Yet it is most likely that my amnesia about these public and communal events reflects the fact that I didn't know where I was, or if I belonged to any political entity, or what bearing the history of Canada or of Quebec, or of their relationship, might have on these events. I was in no position to say where it was I had arrived or what I might think of what was happening in this place. As the crisis unfolded, I was receiving an instant history lesson through the contested media coverage, but the truth was that I was so focused on finding my feet in my graduate program and my teaching at McGill that any larger community and its histories remained distant from me.

In that first year, these events came closer in a way that caught me by surprise. I became aware of a novelist I had not heard of before, or if I had, I had not paid attention. Brian Moore, Belfast-born, Montreal resident for a significant period of time, had returned to the city in October and had quickly written *The Revolution Script*. Much like the celebrated work of Truman Capote and Norman Mailer, Moore's non-fiction novel is written in the style of a thriller, taking the reader behind the news stories and giving a human dimension to figures who would otherwise remain sketches in the media.

I discovered that Moore had worked at the Montreal *Gazette* in the early fifties, knew many journalists and broadcasters, and was well placed to get behind the scenes. But he was also skeptical of the power of the media and of those in power, such as Trudeau, who orchestrated events with professional skill; the young kidnappers were "revolutionaries" in that, powerless in themselves, they could quickly create a revolution by manipulating the media with their manifestos. And the passion he brought to his investigation was really a product of the passion he felt about the sectarian war that had exploded in "Bloody Ulster" and would later express in *Lies of Silence*. In Quebec nationalism, he saw the Catholic nationalism of Northern Ireland, in Pierre Trudeau, a repressive, imperial player, but if he was sympathetic to Quebecers' feelings of being second-class citizens, he was not a supporter of ethnic nationalism or sectarianism. Moore had journalistic skills that allowed him to write a thriller in a few weeks, but my discovery of his other selves, migrant and Irish-Canadian-American novelist, was what slowly became really important for me.

At first, I became aware of him as a successful Canadian novelist. *The Lonely Passion of Judith Hearne*, published in London and then New York, had won him acclaim internationally fifteen years earlier, but it was *The Luck of Ginger Coffey*, set in Montreal, that made him well-known in Canada. It had won literary awards, been made into a successful film, and was studied in English class by Montreal high school students. It is his first novel set outside his native Belfast and tells of the Irish emigrant, Coffey, trying to find his feet in the city. Alert to ways in which the happy-go-lucky Irishman is not well suited to the challenges of emigration, he actually writes an archetypal story of settling in the new place. Moore combines his knowledge of an Irish formation with his knowledge of the city, but in adapting his own experience and giving it fictional form, he reflects on the general condition of migration.

I would later teach this novel in courses at Vanier College, when I began to realize that immigration rather than Irishness was my theme, but at the beginning, hastily assembling a reading list for an Irish Literature course, I included *Judith Hearne* because I though my students would know Moore already. It would be some time before I would think of it as an Irish-Canadian book and realize that I wanted to know how this Irishman had found himself in Montreal: eventually I thought of him as one of those writers — Mavis Gallant another in those years — who would read the city for me, and maybe if I read him well, I could then read myself in the city. But by then, I had also read his continuing investigations of identity and assimilation in novels such as *An Answer from Limbo, I am Mary Dunne, The Mangan Inheritance*, and others, and had realized that for him the process of moving from Ireland to Montreal was only the beginning of a series of migrations in North America and of fictional reflections on the condition of being uprooted from all anchoring beliefs.

The Revolution Script was, to a degree, a reflection on the sixties and on the political and cultural power the media had assumed to shape beliefs and images of belief. One of Moore's finest works came immediately after it, the short novel *Catholics*, in which he examines with striking sympathy the impact on traditional Catholicism of the left-wing "liberation theology," which had challenged, with the support of the media, the very foundation of religious belief. But at the local level of Quebec nationalism, Moore sensed, rightly, that the October Crisis was a symptom and a prophecy of a cultural change orchestrated in a sixties style and yet drawing on traditional xenophobic feeling.

I was a product of the sixties myself, and so I could not see this in the early seventies as I joined in spirit the fashionable turn towards Quebec culture. In my first years at Vanier, I wanted to be *au courant*, as many of my young colleagues did, who were also products of the sixties. I tried to improve my French in conversation classes, although now having to face the fact that my efforts to imitate a Parisian French were misplaced: there was a local accent, and to a degree, a local dialect, *joual*, which the younger generation of educated Québécois favoured as a more authentic expression of their "national" culture. Not only did my poor ear impoverish my second-language French, and betray me as *anglais,* but I was now trapped in other colonialisms, the complex relationship between Quebec and France inside the former French empire. My early francophilia, which had really replaced the Irish language and Irish nationalism as cultural reference points, remained, along with my inherited sympathy for "small nations," and so I was able to join my young colleagues. I went to the great Québécois movies of those years, *Mon oncle Antoine* and *Kamouraska,* and read novels by Marie-Claire Blais and Anne Hébert. I participated wholeheartedly in the *front commun* strike of 1973, a wave of opposition to the Liberal government of Quebec that eventually led to the ousting of that government in 1976 and its replacement by a party committed to the separation of the province from Canada. I voted in my first election since becoming a Canadian citizen, and I voted for the *indépendantiste* party. And there was no question: I would send my children to French school, even though we were not required by law to do so, as were immigrants of other language-backgrounds.

It was in this way, through the language laws limiting choice in the use of languages other than French, that the xenophobic face of Québécois nationalism began to appear more and more; eventually this would transform the student population entering my classrooms: within a decade, most of them would have been educated entirely through French, and so our primary duty became the teaching of language skills rather than literature. But before this happened, I had begun to sort out some of the confusions of my cultural allegiances.

*

Other, practical, challenges came first: how to be a graduate student, how to be a teacher, and how to be a husband and father; and how to do all these things without any plan at all? How to be confident and to know what to do when you feel at sea?

I was hired at Vanier College to teach English, a token Irishman in a department that was designed to mirror the "multicultural mosaic," as I heard it referred to, without really thinking much about it. There was a great variety of English accents in the Department that was being invented at this time in the early seventies. In addition to Canadian, there were British, including Yorkshire and Welsh as well as the BBC accent, Jamaican and Trinidadian, Nigerian and Indian; and American accents from New England, California, the deep South.

We were brought together by a woman whose family had managed to escape from Austria before the Nazi terror began in earnest. She also hired a handful of people whose first language was not English. They, and she, were in favour of teaching literature in translation, for while English was our common language, a high proportion of our students spoke another language at home, most likely, at this stage, a European language, although very soon we would be receiving more and more Latin Americans, Vietnamese and boat people, Lebanese, and, as the decades moved on, Iranians, Haitians, immigrants from all the world's disaster zones.

From the beginning, there was a guiding awareness that the parents of our students would have brought with them other cultures and literatures and that cultural integration, the business we were in, had to include a sensitivity to this. When I was hired, Vanier College had opened only a year earlier, and so I entered into an educational process that was being invented. I was as much learner as teacher, as overwhelmed by the transformation I was undergoing as the parents of my students. My only advantages were that I had a mastery of the English language and I had been inspired by good teachers, so that I had a complete belief in the role and an appreciation of its power and possibilities.

I was hired to teach Irish Literature in a cluster of national literature courses that included West Indian and Slavic among the more obvious offerings of English and American. Many of the students who chose to take these courses were Canadian offspring of immigrants, in my case, of Irish parents or Irish grandparents, and my job was to teach them something of their ancestors' cultural inheritance. The odd thing was I had never actually studied Irish Literature as a separate literary tradition, nor had I thought much about it. Certainly, I had come across the canonical Irish writers in many courses and knew the classic texts, but I had always thought of the poems and stories and novels in the context of the evolution of the traditions of English literature. Even though I had a special appreciation for their work and felt that it spoke to me in an intimate way, the idea of a coherent National Literature had not been part of my thinking — even though, of course, "English Literature" was just that.

I left Ireland as the Northern Troubles revived many nationalistic impulses, and arrived into the orbit of Québécois nationalism, and indeed, of Canadian nationalism, at this time in the seventies, and I noted that in each case, literature was called on to provide some form of national narrative. I felt dubious about this kind of obligation. Even then, I knew that artists find inspiration in relation to their personal needs, and so many literary mentors and models are often chosen from literatures, religions, and histories beyond the obvious cultural borders. In fact, I felt that in many cases, artists owed their power and their accomplishment to such openness, to their resistance to blueprints and their will to find their own, eclectic, way.

At Vanier College, the course that became more important was the other one I was also hired to teach in the beginning: "The Lonely Voice: Modern Short Stories." This title was borrowed from a book on the short story written by Frank O'Connor when, as a successful writer himself, he became a teacher in the United States. His book had essays on Hemingway and Chekhov, Joyce and Mansfield, de Maupassant and Isaac Babel. O'Connor's enthusiasm for their work and for the form itself moved me. All of them, he argued, had found the short story a congenial art form because in their observation of life they noted the isolated, the lonely, the marginal individual. And the short story called for an intense personal response to solitariness: there was no before or after, no historical context, no explanation or alleviation for this common condition.

That was not the story's business. It was, O'Connor argued, more like a poem or a song than a novel. I was won over to his way of seeing the world and the story. I would teach stories by these authors and others, stories from nineteenth-century Russia, contemporary America, North Africa, Canada, France, New Zealand, but where they were set did not matter much; the challenge was to get at the feelings embedded in them. For thirty years I taught short stories, and even though the stories changed over and over and I used different teaching techniques, I continued to use this title for my course. Here, I felt, was a body of literature in which we could find common ground.

Maybe my confidence as a teacher came from my conviction that literature could enlighten in a way that Catholicism had failed to do. I had lost faith in religious clichés and in political clichés too, in all manifestos, doctrines, and arguments. Literary language, the intimate language of individual consciousness, was real, and the teacher's words could coach young readers in the appreciation of its depth. The lonely voice was mine, borrowed, perhaps, from Stephen Dedalus as well as from Frank O'Connor, but like everything else I used for my teacher's mask in those days, it was borrowed unaware. Where else would I have found the confidence to convince my students that the real life of the stories we read together was worth knowing? My love of literature had become my deepest faith, for in it I had found the knowledge that gives imaginative depth to life; maybe it was that faith my students heard when I filled the classroom with words.

★

More than any other author, Brian Moore came to be central to my teaching. I had included *Judith Hearne* in "Irish Literature" and *Ginger Coffey* in "Immigrant Literature." At that early stage, I failed to see that the two novels are very similar, in spite of the careful rendering of settings in Belfast and Montreal. In the opening chapter, Judith Hearne arrives at a new boarding house in Belfast, spends her days wandering the familiar city, her fragile attachments gradually breaking, however, and dreams of new attachments failing, until at the end, she is expelled from the boarding house and ends up in an institution. The new Canadian, Coffey, also has housing problems: he fails to pay his rent, becomes homeless, and winds up living for a time at the YMCA, his marriage failing, and yet he is "lucky," for at the end of the novel he appears to have learned a great deal about himself and developed attitudes which will enable him to settle.

The Lonely Passion of Judith Hearne is an "Irish novel" since it explores with great precision the cultural contexts that have rendered this aging single woman a victim of her own character and attitudes, but it can also be seen as a fiction which reflects Moore's own condition as a migrant. He includes a returned "Yank" and takes much care delineating the attitudes of the locals towards him and to his own difficulties as an emigrant in New York. The tentative steps he and Hearne take towards a relationship reveal the desperate hopes and delusions that envelop them. Coffey too is an emigrant with great delusions and vain hopes, but his buoyant character and his willingness to face harsh home truths reveal him to be a potentially successful immigrant. It is this upbeat ending, no doubt, that endeared the novel to so many Canadian readers, and its comic tone anticipates, perhaps, the memoirs of Frank McCourt, which appealed greatly to immigrant readers worldwide. But Moore's work never had such success, and his elaborate career of fiction writing reveals a lifelong preoccupation with the transitional conditions first treated in these realistic novels.

His exploration of the spiritual conditions of migration engrossed me so that I followed each step of his evolution in his later decades. I felt an intimate connection to the novels, as if they mirrored my own state, but in fact my life was simple in comparison with his. In the final years of World War II, Moore left Belfast and became a clerk in the British Army in North Africa. Although not a soldier, he traveled behind the advancing Allied lines, sometimes close enough to hear the guns and smell the destruction, north through Italy, to France, and into Germany. He saw collaborators shot on the street in Marseille. Auschwitz had just been opened in 1945 when he arrived there, and then he spent two years in Poland with a United Nations Relief organization, as the occupying Soviet army and the Communists established the post-war regime. After a brief return to Belfast, he left for Canada, and in 1948 began a career as a journalist. It was in Montreal that he became a novelist. He settled in the city for a decade, until a Guggenheim Fellowship brought him to New York City for a year, and a process of uprooting began again. A few years later, he moved to California to work in Hollywood with Hitchcock and settled there for the rest of his life.

Over the next decades, the constantly restless novelist spent lengthy periods in Ireland, Montreal, and France, making almost annual visits to these locations of his earlier life, and indeed his novels are set variously in these places or in combinations of them. But if Moore's sense of geographical displacement permeates his fiction, it is equally permeated by a radical doubt about religious and political systems, about the dangers of sectarian and ethnic convictions. In addition, many of the novels reveal deep-seated doubts about the "reality" created by the media and especially television, and even about the evidence of an individual's subjective observations. *An Answer from Limbo*, an early novel set in New York, and including a harsh examination of an exiled Irish writer, prefigures much of what followed, and its title is prophetic. Growing up with the sectarian violence of Belfast, wishing to escape into the historical reality of the larger sphere of Europe at war, the young man grew into a "man of no identity," and yet the restlessness of constant experimentation with fictional styles and genres and narrative voices reflects a lasting commitment to probing the experience of migration. It was the incoherence of the disparate voices, styles and genres that I wanted to understand, to see how life and work intertwined, and it was this that led me to write *The Chameleon Novelist* in the nineties.

*

In the middle of writing *The Chameleon Novelist*, I tuned in one evening to CBC Radio to hear Conor Cruise O'Brien deliver the Massey Lectures. O'Brien's title was "On the Eve of the Millennium." He set the scene with lines from W. B. Yeats's "The Second Coming" – "Things fall apart," etc. It was a characteristic gesture. O'Brien often quoted Yeats, borrowing the gravitas and eloquence of one of the great international figures of his youth in the thirties: for him these words had become the poem of the century.

In my kitchen in Montreal, I sat back and listened to that voice which I had heard so often thirty years before. He moved with ease from the French Revolution to the IRA, from Thomas Jefferson to Bill Clinton and Pope John Paul II, from "sacral nationalism" to the pornographic exploitation by the media of the British royal family, from Greek tragedy to "avoidance rituals" in international diplomacy. The nasal whine had not changed. I had always found it off-putting, but the old excitement was quickly resurrected by his rhetorical power, by the passion and learning that drove his mind, by the snake-like sentences of a worldly thinker.

As I listened, I realized that while the style remained unchanged from the sixties, something was different. Instead of a feeling of intellectual and imaginative liberation, I felt a sense of darkness and intimidation in his words. The gains of Enlightenment thinking – democracy, the rule of law, dispassionate enquiry – were being swept away, he warned, in so many ways that the world would soon be engulfed by bigotry, authoritarianism, and bloodshed. Long before he finished, my mind slipped away. The man I had once assumed was a progressive liberal, perhaps for a time a socialist, had turned into a prophet of global doom. What had happened to the humour and wit, to the sense of writing as performance, as an emblem of the free mind? Was this later voice the true voice of O'Brien that I had failed to notice earlier? Or was he simply an old man now, worn down and rambling? His political career over, he had continued to preach against Irish republicans. Had his obsession blinded him, or dulled him into repetition? After the shock of those radio talks, I found myself wondering why O'Brien once had the power over me that he did.

In the first years after I came to Canada, I began to think of writing about O'Brien. By then the radical sixties and my fantasy of participating in a global movement had been overshadowed by the fury and savagery of daily events in Northern Ireland. O'Brien's attention was focused more and more on the developments there. Soon he became one other voice pushing to be heard above the gunshots and the bombs. I was now moving out of touch with Irish politics and my former friends and colleagues, yet O'Brien's writing remained on my radar for a time. By 1972, when he wrote *States of Ireland*, he was already gripped by the fear that his words would not be powerful enough to wean people from the beat of the "frenzied drum." In the face of relentless republican invocations of ancestral heroism, the subtlety of O'Brien's thinking yielded to the reiteration of a doomsday vision of uncontainable bloodshed. His thinking seemed to be rooted not simply in an aversion to the sectarian element in Irish nationalism, or in his awareness of the slide of Europe in the thirties into war and genocide, the barbarism of his youth, but in some deeper despair about human motivation and the myths that bind ethnic communities.

It was at this point that I considered how a biographer would give shape to O'Brien's life. I imagined myself as his biographer and read everything he had written. It was not finally the coherence of O'Brien's convictions that gripped me, or the insight he could bring to bear on Irish or Quebec nationalism. I wanted to get behind them to the characteristic stance of the thinker, his way of framing his topics, his use of language, his approach to ideas and the people and circumstances in which they had originated. What made him most interesting to me was that he looked out at the world from his rooted Irish experience and then looked back at Ireland from his experience in the wider world. He could be in both places. Now I was in North America, and he was back in Ireland; in some sense I still needed him to be a father to me.

To write an account of his life and ideas in the seventies, when he was an active politician, even a minister in government, would be an act of public homage at a time when I didn't want to be anyone's disciple. In any case, I failed to write it: my false start in mapping a life shrank into an article in an obscure journal. It would have been a bad biography, simply echoing his ideas and his language. When I look back now, I know that I lacked the confidence to take on a biographical study of such a large figure, so well known, and so overwhelmingly himself. Lacking a voice of my own, or the courage to see through O'Brien, I could have performed an act of ventriloquism. Perhaps I should have written the book, fully aware of such ironies and contradictions. Perhaps it would have given me the means to go far enough beyond my country-boy reticence, my colonial deference, my ex-Catholic disenchantment, to absorb the confident, adversarial style of O'Brien. I did not need to practice that style at his expense; maybe it was the rhetorical strategies I could have learned. After all, I was living in Canada, and my experience was going to be different. I did not need to be adopted by O'Brien any longer, or to keep him as my idol, although I did something I now find even more significant: when I became a father for the first time, I named my son after him.

Years later, by the time I was sitting in my kitchen listening to O'Brien's radio talks, the writing of biography had become a way of affirming my deepest convictions about the slow growth of an individual life. The courage to speak as a character in my own book came slowly, and I realized that this had always been a problem in my efforts to write. I had been intimidated by father figures whose presences I had magnified. My father lacked authority in his own character; all I knew was that he was a silent man and that I was in real danger of following his path. Who dares to speak? And at what age?

Having won the confidence to say so much that I believed to be true about Brian Moore's life, I could also admit to what I did not know, and could not know. For the first time, I felt free to write in a voice that was close to my own, to the voice I had discovered in growing from being the son of my father to being the father of my own sons.

EIGHT

In my first year in North America, it dawned on me that the revolution I felt I had joined in Dublin was not the real revolution, or, at least, it was only a part of the larger upheaval of the sixties. The student revolution, the anti-Vietnam movement, the New Left, I had embraced them all enthusiastically, but now I discovered, to my discomfort, that sex too was part of politics, that the Revolution was against all forms of repression and authoritarianism, and that sexual freedom was the ultimate utopian absolute. It must have been this realization that led me to devote so much of the next years to reading D. H. Lawrence.

This revolution seemed to have been born in California, but Lawrence, formulating his doctrines of liberation in Italy with his lover, Frieda, had anticipated much of this fifty years earlier. His mystical sensualism was expressed in the paradisal symbolism of flowers, but everyone seemed to know it was sex he was writing about. While some of Lawrence's high-minded interpreters spoke of "the priest of love" and his "love ethic," others, less sentimental, wrote of a fierce Oedipal conflict, of ingrained Puritanism, and a purgation of shame. In North America, in the sixties, the public exhibitions of sexual freedom asserted that if only sex in all its variations were no longer hidden from public view, everyone and the whole culture of materialism and militarism would be cleansed.

It was certainly a revolutionary subversion of every principle on which Catholic Ireland was founded and with which I had been indoctrinated. The once-banned author of *Lady Chatterley's Lover* and *The Rainbow* had now become an icon not only of free love but of the liberation the sixties offered, although leading writers of the Women's Liberation movement had their doubts about him. Why was I holding back on Lawrence? What young man wouldn't identify with the desire for freedom from middle-class and Christian inhibitions, from goal-oriented, repressive ambitions, and in favour of rehabilitating the instinctual, the "natural man"?

The further reaches of the sexual revolution — the purgation of inhibition, the absolute of the pleasure principle — had a psychedelic glow. Revolutionary philosophies (Marcusian, Maoist, anarchist), the "joys" of sex, Eastern mysticism — all the utopian impulses seemed to have trajectories that merged at infinity. The "mysteries of the organism" that had to be released seemed to me to have more to do with the chemical bombardment of the brain than with a liberation that I could manage.

Without knowing it, perhaps, I had cooperated earlier in keeping even the simplest of pleasures invisible — invisible in a certain way even from myself. The most difficult part of my adolescent revolt, it had seemed to me, was a doctrinal one, focused on the claims of the Church to have the monopoly on truth; little did I realize that its ethos had already infected my emotional and sensual life, so that to declare "I do not believe in Catholicism" or "I am no longer a practising Catholic" was only a superficial liberation, a limited, intellectual revolt. And yet there was a major part of me that felt oppressed, or maybe frightened by a vague prospect of where this interest in Lawrence was taking me.

Could it be that it was not Lawrence and his visions but scholarship itself that was oppressive? I had been brought up in a culture of prophets, zealots, and great men through whose agency, we had believed, the Truth could be revealed. My sense of oppression may have come from that constant self-discipline required by dispassionate scholarly work, the cautious holding back, the deferred commitment to certainty that makes the future a permanent hypothesis, when it is a breakthrough to the Truth that one still craves. The worship of prophets, heroes, and intellectual mentors, the yearning to identify fully and escape from doubt, to have one's beliefs and sense of self mapped out, is both tempting and frightening.

I was oppressed by my own anxious desire to be a scholar, and the nature of the subject I found myself trapped with, the novels of D. H. Lawrence, made that desire even more anxious. How could a reader like me who had found intense personal pleasure and a stabilizing sense of purpose in literature take the holistic vision of Lawrence's art and measure it out with teaspoons? Either I allowed the act of reading, the pleasure of aesthetic experience in all its individual manifestations, to become an act of faith in a qualitatively different life, or I became a detached and dull scholar for whom love and appreciation were of secondary importance. I could not bring myself to betray Lawrence's fire; neither could I allow myself to be cowed into ventriloquism by a zealot.

*

"All religions I think have the same inner conception," Lawrence wrote to an Irishman named Gordon Campbell in

December 1914, "with different expressions." Campbell had given him the draft of a novel, but Lawrence, midway through *The Rainbow* at this time, dismissed his friend's work: "Why don't you seek out the whole of the Celtic Vision, instead of messing about talking of Ireland." I was surprised that the novelist would use an expression like "messing about" – it sounded so contemporary – but even more, I was startled by a defensive feeling that Lawrence was challenging me, for I had recently left Ireland and it was still the only place I knew very much about.

When I read the letter, and *The Rainbow*, and *Sons and Lovers*, and everything by Lawrence – his work had become the subject of my research at McGill – it was not so long since I had abandoned the Catholic "whole" of my childhood. "It is very beautiful," Lawrence wrote of his new religious vision, "and a very great conception which, when one feels it, satisfies one, and one is at rest." But I could not fall under the spell of his prophecies. I could not feel this "rest" in Lawrence's work, or in my own life. I was in search of my own kind of liberation, a boy from the country, adrift for some time already, trying to hold on to a tentative version of scholarship as scaffolding for my skepticism. I was not ready for another holistic vision, even if it was called "Celtic."

From elementary school years, we were encouraged to think of ourselves as Celts, and I knew that Yeats and other Irish writers had drawn major inspiration from the rich mythology of gods and heroes. An explicit kind of political, religious, and cultural identity, a version of "de-anglicization," had been attached to this Celtic mythology since the nineteenth century, and, in my schooldays, nationalist zealots had already dominated the cultural discourse for generations. They too seemed to be inspired by a vision of a "whole," not the geographical whole of the island of Ireland, necessarily, but a sense of spiritual wholeness in the pure and essential idea of Irishness. In adolescence, however, I read Joyce's portrait of an Irish Catholic lad in search of something more than orthodoxy. Disillusioned and disenchanted, I was encouraged by the protective arrogance of Stephen Dedalus.

A little guiltily, I left Ireland for Canada; the study of literature seemed to be altogether more manageable than the abstractions of liberation and justice, or the commitments demanded by the bloody politics of the streets. I would become a scholar. I would maintain the necessary detachment from the slippery slopes of zealotry, of which, I was inclined to think, there was too much in Ireland. Literary scholarship had its own visions of perfection, the purity of expression, the perfection of style, the exhaustive weighing of detail. Scholars left no stone unturned, but to what end? If truth was no longer revealed by oracles, scriptures, and zealots, what was it? Something discovered in a library? As a professional student, I had to believe so. I did not want to be respected for the intensity and clarity of my political commitment, but for the imaginative pressure of my attention to literary style.

Little did I know how out of step with the times I was in my loss of faith, how old-fashioned in my Joycean wish to be freed from all mythologies, for the sixties would live on, its promises of liberation proliferating, especially within the university, and in particular in the ways literature would come to be studied there. It would have been easier later on if I had been able to throw in my lot with early manifestations of fervent deconstruction, the progressive camp in the culture wars, as these bitter struggles would be known in the eighties, but I could not. It was in Montreal, in the seventies, that my mind became oppressed by Lawrence's mythology of "resurrection" and his mystical faith in "the whole." In a way I could not articulate or even recognize, the novelist kept open my rawest, unresolved inheritance from my formation in Ireland

*

Gordon Campbell's reaction to Lawrence's abuse is not recorded, but the messianic novelist pressed his case for not wasting one's life with local matters on another writer in the months following. He got to know E.M. Forster in January 1915. Forster knew a great deal about "the whole" of Indian religions, for he had read widely on the history and culture of Islam and Hinduism, and he had lived in India for a year. He was less impressed by Lawrence's abrasive preaching about sex and politics than by the delicacy of his attention to nature and the sheer force of his visionary conviction. Although Forster had written *Howards End*, a "condition of England" novel, earlier in his career, he knew that the psychological and metaphysical realm Lawrence was attempting to capture in his fiction went far beyond that, and he wanted to follow him; in fact, he had already attempted to do so after his return from India. He had begun a new novel but would not be able to complete *A Passage to India* for almost a decade more.

What was remarkable to me about Forster as a reader — so remarkable that he became a central part of my work on Lawrence from this point on — was that he had to overcome major resistance in himself to be able to speak out. "Prophetic fiction,"

Forster wrote, "seems to have definite characteristics. It demands humility and the absence of the sense of humour . . . it gives us the sensation of a song or of sound." Lawrence's demand for humility is what Forster learned to respond to, and he learned it directly when he was brought face to face with the novelist.

In 1927 Forster recalled that encounter. "Nothing is more disconcerting than to sit down, so to speak, before your prophet, and then suddenly to receive his boot in the pit of your stomach. 'I'm damned if I'll be humble after that,' you cry, and so lay yourself open to further nagging. Also the subject matter of the sermon is agitating – hot denunciations or advice – so that in the end you cannot remember whether you ought or ought not to have a body, and are only sure that you are futile." This is Forster's recollection of how Lawrence had treated him in 1915, and this startling revelation was reassuring to me because it articulated so vividly my own feelings of being overpowered by Lawrence's words. Lawrence had indeed bullied Forster and humiliated him, and had analyzed in blunt terms the root causes of his ineffectual personality. He had urged Forster to resurrect himself, partly by becoming sexually assertive, and to join him in creating "a perfect community that would regenerate the world." The irony was not lost on Forster that Lawrence's idea of sexual regeneration was strictly heterosexual, for already Forster had found such a "perfect community" among friends from Cambridge and would go on to expand his homosexual community.

I discovered how Forster had read Lawrence, and also how Lawrence had read Forster, and how Lawrence's imagination had made use of that reading. I became a scholar with something new to say. In this process I did find a way out of my oppression and out of the hole of self-doubt in which I had buried myself. Although my academic work was praised for its originality and its contribution to understanding Lawrence's critical imagination, I no longer believed in it. In the end, I had grown to appreciate both writers in certain ways, but I had wearied of them. I no longer wanted to read them. My scholarship was at a dead end.

Deep down, by becoming a scholar, I felt I had sidestepped the issues. I was still perhaps the country boy in awe of the accomplishments of others, lacking the fierce will of that other country boy, Lawrence, to clear the space for himself. Forster had known what he needed to take from Lawrence and how to keep the space clear. I was left with this conundrum of how to read, how to surrender oneself to the pleasure of being inside someone else's world, to assent to its truth, and how at the same time to affirm one's own self, one's own separate and distinctive truth.

*

My first published writing in Canada was an appreciation of *The Leavetaking*, John McGahern's novel of a day in the life of a man who must leave Ireland. The novel, together with his earlier books, *The Barracks*, *The Dark*, and *Nightlines*, became, in my settling in Montreal, the most deeply felt books I had ever read; they were books of the farming world I had grown up in and left behind, and the Dublin I had known, and yet McGahern had revealed in that small world a universe of meaning.

His four volumes of fiction, so well known in England and Ireland, were almost unknown in North America. This was the mid-seventies, before the boom in contemporary Irish culture, which was indirectly promoted by the slaughter in the North that won headlines worldwide and provoked a curiosity about its background. McGahern's work was not diagnostic in political or historical terms, but it did open up darknesses of faith and violence, of terror and fierce despair, of personal isolation and censorship, of vulnerability and mortality, of love lost and won. His images of Ireland came to me with a such visceral immediacy and poetic power that I can no longer say to what degree McGahern's fiction has coloured my whole way of seeing Ireland and seeing myself. Certainly, my admiration for his work led me to think of it as an articulation of an incontrovertible truth about life; in his books, he had found a way of using language that was beyond speech and silence; his novels and stories had a visionary aura, although few visionary artists have their feet as firmly planted on the ground as McGahern.

My commitment to reading from an early age led me to think of writing as the medium that would allow me to be more precisely myself – although to escape from cliché in writing was a goal I could not achieve; my dream of writing was a dream of control. Yet because I had placed such a high value on the poetic, I seemed to be forever stuck in silence, my only recourse to point admiringly towards the fiction of McGahern, to suggest, perhaps, why it ought to be appreciated and valued.

My "Note" on *The Leavetaking* was my first effort to find a way to do this. Fifteen years after that first note, I wrote a book about all of McGahern's fiction and attempted to map the evolution of his imaginative engagement in the sequence of novels and stories of his first thirty years as a writer. It is surely ironic that even though my book includes no biographical information and does not in any way attempt to show a connection between the fiction and his life, I did indeed learn that my insight into the fiction derived from an intense and unconscious awareness of the life that informed it – the life that is hidden in circumstances. I realized that perhaps what I had been able to trace reflected in some way an allegory of my own inner life. The most intense reading, as the most intense writing, comes out of our hidden life, and so it is that writing about reading is a form of memoir.

*

Some time after this, I realized that Lawrence's myths and fables reflect a desire to return to an Eden of sensual contentment and peace. He had superimposed Frieda's libertarian philosophies of sex on his happy moments with her in the first few years in their Italian exile. He returned to London in 1914, certain that his ideas could become the basis for a new social order. Later, as the slaughter and censorship of the war years drove him to the edge of madness, the idyll with Frieda seems to have fallen away, to be replaced by more strident theorizing. The fictions he imagined out of that first experience were written with the desperation of memory, the fury to create in the future what was already lost.

I recognized now what I shared with him, the experiences of loss and exile. Over the years, Montreal became home for me, and in my settling, I gradually moved on from thinking of my life in those terms. And yet, even as the circumstances of life become more ordinary, the mysterious depths take on their own shape. Perhaps it was this, as middle age came quickly toward me, that allowed me to discover again how to read

Lawrence. The farms of his Nottinghamshire and Derbyshire reproduced my own childhood farm in Ireland. He never did make his peace with urban ways of life, and in his hideouts off the beaten track, in Italy, Australia, and America, he remained a country boy. His intimacy with the hedgerows and the meadows, the trees and the animals had nourished his descriptions of a nineteenth-century landscape that seemed familiar to me as an image of my first home in County Clare.

Ireland and my childhood on the farm moved far away as the years were added to years in this city of immigrants, in this new home. But "messing about talking of Ireland" did become a way of reading my life, as indeed messing about talking of England became Lawrence's constant inspiration as he lived elsewhere. Learning to read the fiction of John McGahern was a training in reading myself, and I realized too that an English novelist like Lawrence could have helped me in that reading, if I had not been intimidated by his hectoring tone. Rather than a utopian visionary whose "whole" would regenerate industrial and urban England, Lawrence was a writer of elegies for the landscapes of his childhood, forever a writer of memoirs.

NINE

Our first autumn in this old house in the centre of Montreal, I planted a Norway maple in the front garden, and it is now taller than the house. Some lighter branches gently touch my bedroom window, and often the sun shimmering on the leaves is the first thing I see in the morning. I chose a Norway maple because my neighbour, Attila, had just planted one. He had fled Hungary as a teenager in 1956, before the uprising was crushed, and was adopted in France before making his way to Montreal. Side by side our trees have grown, their countless yellow leaves the last to fall after the reds and oranges have come down.

Our single trees here on the street are like scattered reminders of what envelops Mount Royal, which begins its steep rise just a block away. Within minutes I can be on the mountain among the trees. My first winter in the city, I was persuaded to try cross-country skiing, and so, equipped with two narrow wooden skis, I tried my luck on the trails that encircle the summit. I persevered for some winters and introduced my young sons to the magic of zipping through snow-laden trees, although, of course, they soon wanted to go for the downhill action on the real mountains in the Laurentians or the Appalachians, an hour or two away by car.

But it is as a place for walking on the gravelled avenues that I have always loved the wooded mountain, in all seasons, at least until the snow and the skiers take over. I walk on the mountain with my wife, my daughter, with friends, or even alone. Unlike many who go to the mountain to picnic in family groups, or take in the sun, or exercise vigorously, or have a romantic interlude, or just relax away from the traffic and the commerce, I go there for the trees themselves.

On the mountain in the heart of Montreal, I am back in the country, walking among old trees as I did in my first years in County Clare beside Lough Derg. The lanes around our farm were often cathedrals of greenery, the dense hedgerows of willows and alders, whitethorns and hazels, which cut off the view of the fields on either side, rising up with old columns of beech, ash, or sycamore. Along the lakeside, woodlands had renewed themselves for centuries.

The lanes led to the village and to the school, and I would wander under the overarching branches that had been there forever, or as long as the lanes had been there, or maybe longer, for who is to say if the original lanes curved around the trees or if the trees grew up along the lane. If I came upon an acorn, or a chestnut fallen open, its gleaming mahogany shell set off against the mother of pearl lining of its husk, I would think I had found gold. And my brother and I would bore a hole through the chestnut, thread a string through with a knot at the end, and play vicious games of conkers.

One of my earliest memories is of the low-hanging branch of a huge chestnut tree that occupied a central spot in the large field that encircled our house. My father sat me up on it and gently bounced it up and down. The excitement must have been intense for it is an indelible part of my childhood, and I often returned to it later under my own steam. I think it may well have been there in the days of my father's childhood too, and so for him, in those moments, time stopped, the pleasure his and mine, but now there is an empty space, for the chestnut came down in a storm some years ago.

Storms. The wind in the trees. That's the other memory, possibly an even earlier one. My mother feared the wind. She expected a falling branch to hit the old house or slates to be blown off the roof. But I remember all the stormy nights I lay in bed listening to the gusty creaking of the trees or, more often, to the soothing constant hush through the leaves that sent me off to sleep. Listening to the storm outside was tense drama for my parents, but the trees that enveloped the house were all comforting to me.

I graduated from having my own house in the fork of the old chestnut tree, and from other structures built with my brother in other trees, to the woods by the lakeside, to the true adventure in unknown lands. Down there, I knew the illegal eel fishers camped in secret, for my father sometimes helped them out, and when my mother read us *Robinson Crusoe*, it was an entirely real scenario to me. I imagined myself living in the woods, even running away from family troubles to my own lost place. In my father's childhood, a soldier had deserted from the British army during World War I and had lived in those woods for some time. This was the kind of secluded place the Virgin Mary might appear, if you were holy enough, like the children in Lourdes or Fatima.

Mount Royal is not, of course a secluded place where fantasies of a dreamy child might prosper; it is next to the downtown core, rising up behind the McGill campus, and now entirely surrounded by the city, which occupies the whole island and spills across the river to the north and south shore suburbs.

The French and Catholic presence was established first, and that is clear in the name Jeanne Mance, Montreal's first nurse and founder of the Hôtel-Dieu Hospital on the slope of Mount Royal at the edge of the ghetto. It has not been much more than a century, however, since the city expanded up from the river as far as the university and the hospital, and brownstone houses like ours were built in terraces on farmers' fields. Just a few blocks over was the First Presbyterian Church of Montreal, built around the same time, for, as the names of these streets reveal, it was mostly a Scottish development: Hutchison, Lorne, Aylmer. It lasted less than a century. The Church was converted into condominiums twenty-five years ago, soon after we bought this run-down house, for it was then that the neighbourhood – the McGill ghetto, largely cheap rooming houses with a floating population and sprawling apartment buildings that were student warrens – began to gain a new downtown life.

This little enclave was always the poor neighbour of the Golden Square Mile, and had fallen into material neglect and a rather grubby lifestyle, like so many inner city neighbourhoods in the mid twentieth century. It is just minutes away from the large department stores on St. Catherine Street, no longer known as Morgan's, Eaton's, Simpsons, and Ogilvy's, as they were when I arrived here; from the Museum of Modern Art and other museums and galleries on Sherbrooke Street; from Central Station and Christchurch Cathedral; from all the landmarks of downtown – the downtown of formerly Anglo-Montreal, it should be said; a French centre, largely an entertainment centre of theatres, bars and clubs, is a little to the east. But this French centre is not far either from our ghetto, a few minutes walk to Place des Arts and now the expanded Quartier des Spectacles, and in my time here, shopping and entertainment, English and French and immigrant Montrealers have merged; and downtown has become an integrated space. The ghetto, in its revival, has also become that kind of mixed neighbourhood, although the mixture of Scottish and French streetnames suggests that it probably always was culturally mixed.

But if we are now at the heart of a large, multicultural city, the mountain was once a secluded place, the highest point on the island, a vantage point for observing anyone approaching by the St. Lawrence River. There was a settlement called Hochelaga, of Iroquois people, almost certainly located on this lower slope of the mountain where our street now stands. Jacques Cartier came here for a few days in 1535 on his second voyage of exploration, and the friendly aboriginals led him to the top of the mountain, which he named Mont Royal in honour of the French King. When he returned in 1541, however, the village of Hochelaga with its cultivated fields and the villagers, perhaps a few thousand people, had disappeared. There was no clear indication of what had happened, nor have archaeologists and historians solved the riddle. The Iroquois were somewhat nomadic, moving on when agricultural land seemed to become less fertile, but it is also thought that they may have been exterminated by the warlike Hurons, or rival Iroquois, or by disease. At any rate, Hochelaga vanished, and the mountain remained a wilderness until the town of Ville-Marie was set up a century later, in 1642, by de Maisonneuve; it soon lost its name in favour of Montreal.

The story of the first encounters between French explorers and the native people is told in large wall-panels close to the ceiling of "the chalet." This large hall is situated at the top of the mountain, set back from the lookout or belvedere that offers magnificent views over the city and off to the mountains in Vermont and New York State. For a few years, a chamber music festival was held at the chalet, and when we used to come out at the end of the concert, we could look out over the illuminated city before descending the long stairways that lead down to McGill campus and home. The extraordinary vision of city fathers at the end of the nineteenth century forced the development of the city to go around the base of the mountain, and so it remained as a wild park, lightly landscaped by Frederick Law Olmsted, who had designed Central Park in Manhattan.

This mountain is an essential part of my daily life here. I can catch a glimpse of it from my bedroom window. I get my first sense of the day's weather by looking in that direction, as well as the seasonal changes, the coming of spring as the trees gradually turn green, of autumn as it is illuminated with yellow, orange, and red maples, and the first large snowfalls that leave it covered in Christmas trees; the first snowstorms are always exciting, fresh snow glittering everywhere under a blue sky, but soon the irrevocable setting in of winter is marked by a mountain that takes repeated storms until it looks frozen solid and a grayish-white.

*

The mountain is for me both city and country. The history of human settlements around its base is a history of expansions, contractions, and refurbishments, of the way cities accommodate change, with welcome, with regret, and finally with acceptance. I am here in the midst of social, economic and political evolutions, in a prosperous North American city, in the very heart of downtown, a site of pleasure, wealth and business, and yet I am in this ghetto with a view to the mountain. It all seems right for me.

In my first urban years, as a student in Dublin, I could never imagine myself living in suburbia, moving off and settling down there in a neighbourly community, travelling an hour each day to and from work in the centre, and when I came to Montreal, I could not imagine either that I would end up in a suburb. As my children grew up here, it sometimes seemed that suburbs had all the advantages for children, that life would be so much easier, so many facilities would be available to them, so many friends, so many organized activities. And there would be parents who were struggling with all the same issues of schools, teachers, and sports teams, who's in, who's out, who's taking care of what, all hands on deck. As we stubbornly resisted the move away from the ghetto, we sometimes wondered if we were depriving them of a proper childhood, depriving ourselves of proper neighbours and of a community. Would everyone feel more keenly that they belonged, that this place was home, not simply a house on a downtown street in a part of the city where thousands of people lived temporarily while they attended McGill? Could this house be a family home to which one could be attached?

It was never intended as an experiment in raising a family. I had my first apartment on the corner of Durocher and Milton, and then when my wife came, we moved one block over to Hutchison. When our son began to crawl and stand and then take an interest in the balcony – we were on the twelfth floor –

it was time to move, and we did, to Sainte-Famille, just a few doors north of Milton. When our second son was born years later, we moved over a block, to Jeanne-Mance, and then when our daughter came, we finally bought this house on Lorne, again about the same number of houses up from Milton. This central artery of the ghetto is not a commercial street for the most part, but I have walked on this street every day for all the years I have been in the city. From all these various addresses, I have walked along a section of Milton, to Park Avenue to the shops or the cinema; to McGill, to the library or for meetings, or to take my children to daycare; or towards the metro to travel to my job, or to go downtown. And now that I am not so rushed, I make sure to go anywhere in the general downtown direction by passing through the McGill campus, a park I can appreciate now for its beautiful trees and Victorian buildings.

In spite of some ugly apartment buildings of the fifties and sixties, Milton Street itself has some beautiful buildings and small terraces – the home of the Russian trade mission from the end of the nineteenth century, for instance, and a magnificent redbrick apartment building facing the end of our street, with an inner courtyard and an air that always recalls to me the many beautiful redbrick buildings in London or Dublin from this period. But Milton has a landmark that is just about coequal with my time living in Montreal. Midway along the street, a small Chinese laundry, as it was when I came, very soon became The Word bookstore – second-hand books, mostly literature, and academic textbooks at the appropriate time of the year, but one knows that antiquarian books and first editions are just out of sight. The store has been run by my neighbour and friend, Adrian, for all those years – he and his wife, Luci, created it after a summer selling books in small towns in British Columbia from the back of a van in which they lived, and at first they operated out of their apartment next door, the business in their living room identifiable by a poster of George Bernard Shaw. It was not so much a hippie place they created as a literary-art place, packed with books from floor to ceiling, and if you didn't find what you wanted, Adrian would slip upstairs where the loft was packed, and if it wasn't there, it might be in his basement on Aylmer Street, and if he failed to find it, as he rarely did, he would have it for you the next time you came in.

The Word has been a haven for McGill students for more than a generation, and for many literary friends from all over the city. Its Christmas parties are legendary, its tiny standing-room space packed by people picking up a glass of mulled wine and amazing sweet nibbles and battling to get out onto the sidewalk, often withstanding fierce winter temperatures, breaths clouding the air, until making their way inside for more food and drink. It has been a haven in a particular way for me, because when my son was preschool or elementary school age and we were walking home, we would stop off to take a look at the children's books in the corner, and then as he became more independent, he would stop off himself and was often found ensconced in an art deco armchair in that corner, helping himself to the books and keeping Adrian entertained with his opinions and stories. It was here that many of his favourite children's books were discovered, and, of course, this corner was discovered too by our next two children, for Adrian was always welcoming and loved children.

Recently, when I was walking to our house with my granddaughter, I mentioned to her that one day I would take her on a tour of the ghetto and show her all the places her dad lived in when he was growing up, and she asked me, "Can we go to the bookstore where he sat in the corner and read?"

★

Milton Street has been the main street of my place for all these decades, named, I assume, after the author of *Paradise Lost*. It runs between Saint-Laurent and the eastern gates of the McGill campus, and is often crowded with bicycles and students. It makes a certain sense that it was named thus by literary-minded professors at the university, not even, perhaps, for his authorship of the great epic but for his defence of Protestant liberty of conscience. The university was founded in the early nineteenth century on land given by James McGill, one of the Scottish barons who built the commercial life of the city.

A short way north of here, along Saint-Urbain, is the heart of the old Jewish ghetto settled more than a century ago. There was never a ghetto in the European sense, but there was a neighbourhood where refugees from Russia and Poland created a Jewish village. Saint-Laurent is also known as "The Main" because along part of its length, it was the main commercial street of the village. The history of Montreal in the twentieth century is in part the story of the success of that community as the children born in the ghetto went out and prospered in business and the arts. Saul Bellow spent part of his childhood here before his family moved to Lachine and then Chicago, and Leonard Cohen's parents had moved out before he was born. Most of the talented Jewish youth, however, did not walk along Milton Street to the McGill gates, for there was a quota on Jewish admissions right up to 1960 – so much for the Scottish Enlightenment and freedom of conscience. Also north of the McGill ghetto are other ethnic neighbourhoods that formed between the French working-class areas to the east and the prosperous enclave of Outremont. Greek and Portuguese immigrants came in great numbers after the war, and farther off is Little Italy, in fact not so little for there is a large Italian population in many parts of Montreal now. And, older than any of these urban villages was the Irish neighbourhood near the river, in Pointe-Saint-Charles and Griffintown, dating from the mid nineteenth century. Impoverished tenants and landless workers fleeing the Great Famine first settled here, and they were joined by later immigrants. Their streetnames are still there: St Patrick, Hibernia, Dublin.

I did not seek out the descendants of this Irish community when I arrived, no more than I sought out the largest community of all, *les Québécois*. My ghetto was McGill and my main street Milton, and so it has remained.

When I look out from the back of this old house and across the lane, I cannot avoid looking into the elaborate garden created by my neighbour, Luigi. It is an urban garden, its flowering shrubs and vines tended with care, but the plants take their place around an elaborate fountain and various stoneworks. The redbrick wall on the back of his house is adorned with stone masks and there are also stone figures around the walkways. I like to think Luigi has brought his first impressions of the perfect Mediterranean garden with him, as I have created some kind of recollection of a Clare countryside. Unlike Luigi's garden, which catches sun all summer long, my space is mostly in shadow, and so, twenty-five years ago I set down irregular fieldstones and let moss and other small plants grow between and over them, the stone yard surrounded by mature ferns imported from the countryside, and the fences and brick walls covered in Virginia creeper that reaches up towards the overhanging trees. I like to think that this quiet bower of greenery is a marriage of the Burren on the Atlantic coast of Clare and the rain-sodden ditches of the farm.

*

"Margaret, are you grieving / Over Goldengrove unleaving?" It is autumn, and when I walk up on the mountain at this time of the year, these words of Hopkins memorized in schooldays come into my head. The maples are golden and red and yellow and shades of all these luminous colours blend with the greens of trees not yet turned; the sky is cloudless blue, the sunlight shining through to create pools of gold on the arcaded avenues. Such natural beauty in the centre of the city is a great gift, the colours splashing on city streets and creeping up old greystone and redbrick houses, down onto my own garden fence. There is no reason at all to grieve. The season is one of the wonders of the world.

Why do I recall those words of Hopkins now? Maybe it's because the poem is called "Spring and Fall" and, now that I rarely say autumn, I'm amused by the way the bookish priest-poet, who never came to North America, could play with the word "fall." I suspect it is more than that, for the poem ends with the grim line, "It is Margaret you mourn for," and my deep pleasure in the here and now, the play of light and colour, is shadowed by the gloom that withers everything.

My memory for the words may be embedded by the doctrines that enveloped me in my Catholic childhood, the great Fall the start of all the other falls into sin, everything on this earth somehow the shoddy second best after the garden in the sky. Those gloomy teachings wanted to reiterate that our end is everything, present in our beginning and in our every moment, for we know not the day nor the hour of our individual end or the end of the world. This poem is the exact opposite of another by Hopkins we learned: "Glory be to God for dappled things." That is the one I should be remembering, I tell myself.

Today all is changed. Overnight, many leaves blew down and Chemin Olmsted is inches deep in reds, oranges, and yellows. After my wife and I climbed up to this carriage path to start the circle, our feet shuffling through the fallen leaves, she remarked "This reminds me of the first time you took me out, and we walked home through the leaves by Stephen's Green." It wasn't the colours, it was simply the shuffling sound of our feet that echoed, that brought back a long-buried instant, a flash of memory that lit up that whole evening from so long ago.

It was in late October 1969. I had asked her out to see *Man and Superman* at the Gaiety Theatre. We had met briefly at a party, introduced by a mutual friend My invitation had fallen like manna: Peter O'Toole was the leading actor. Peter O'Toole! In the flesh, although far off from the seats I could afford on the balcony. She would go anywhere to see him, as she would much later to see Jeremy Irons, although I can't see that I have anything in common with either. It was Peter O'Toole who changed my life on that October night at the Gaiety Theatre. The talk over coffee afterwards at Robert Roberts may have been decisive too. At any rate, by the time we were making our way through the leaves en route to her bedsitter on Upper Leeson Street, the threshold into the future had been crossed, the fire had flared up. The fallen leaves are, of course, not "goldengrove unleaving." They are indelibly imprinted on my wife's living inner history, forever associated with this first step in the transformation of her life.

Everything became possible after that walk through the fallen leaves, although I did put a foot wrong many times. Maybe the most important thing was that we no longer believed that our garden was second rate, for we believed that our goldengrove could be as beautiful as any in the sky. We could create our own avenues and plant our own trees – which we did, although far from St. Stephen's Green. And so, while most of our first year together was spent around the Green, and in and out over the Grand Canal, when it was time for the leaves to fall again, I had actually left the city altogether, and we would soon settle in Montreal.

And so, we never again played in those leaves on the north side of the Green; the leaves of October 1969 are unique in my wife's memory. In that rustle on the mountain, she became young again, starting out on the avenue to here.

TEN

A dream came true at the end of the eighties. For years I had hoped to spend a long period of time in France, and then the possibility arose of teaching for a year at the Université de Caen, in Normandy. As a family, we had many memorable and worthwhile adventures, but in the end, the truth of the dream was not what I had expected.

Fermée comme une huître was a common characterization of Normans, a woman from Provence told me with some irritation, and I discovered one day that my dictionary translated *un fin Normand* as "a shrewd fellow." This preference for minding one's own business seemed to be mirrored in the sullen design of the centuries-old Norman farmhouse we were staying in at the end of the year. A passerby could look in a narrow gateway on a cobblestone yard, but the high stone structure turned its solid back to the road. All windows faced inwards.

Clearly, this was not a château. The farmers of a few hundred years ago had no use for the display of a little avenue with trees framing an aristocratic façade. Many of those châteaux still survived and prospered in the region – survived intact with grace, it seemed, through centuries of wars, revolutions, and military campaigns. Whatever historical interpretation I might try to elicit from the architecture of our farmhouse, one thing was certain: its existence as a home was coming to an end.

It may have been the aging of Monsieur and Madame

Dragon and the fact that they had no heir to take over the farm which led them to abandon it, or perhaps it was that the buildings themselves were impractical for the business of contemporary farming. They had abandoned it a year before when they were offered live-in jobs at the prosperous stud farm across the road. Horses from Normandy were doing well at the bloodstock sales in England. Madam Dragon still came each day to feed a blind and disabled old dog that was tied up in a shed; she referred to him gently as her *pauvre bonhomme*, and then went to the barn to feed the rabbits that were being raised in cages. Her daily visit was the only disturbance in our quiet tenancy.

I remember sitting in a beach chair in the middle of that overgrown yard, reading passages from *The Enigma of Arrival*. Its picture of Naipaul's isolation in Wiltshire was strangely appropriate to my own location and to my state of mind. There was the coincidence of his withdrawal from London to a previously unknown countryside, and his gradual discovery through familiarity of the contours of the landscape, its lanes and trees and houses. The first section of the book captured that slow sense of beginning again in a new place, as if one had to become like Adam to truly notice what was there. Naipaul's memoir, which he subtitled "a novel in five parts," became for me for a brief period a kind of prayer book.

At the end of June we had left the house on the inner harbour in Port en Bessin that had been our home since September. Our landlord there, Pierre Labbe, was a stocky fisherman with his own small trawler, *Le Risque-tout*. Each morning when he returned from the fishing grounds, he and his mate tied up the *chalutier* between the house and the co-op where the morning fish auctions were held, and so we often greeted him on our way to the *boulangerie* or on the children's way to school. In the first weeks, as we tried to read the signs of life in this small fishing port, we noticed that, unlike the other fishermen, our landlord did not repair to the *La Rotonde* each morning for cognac or *pastis*. His wife picked him up at 9.30 in the small Citroën van, and they drove out the road towards Bayeux. Soon we learned that he had recently bought a small farm with an attractive new house on the main road. In February, *Le Risque-tout* went down just outside the harbour during a nasty winter storm. Monsieur Labbe and his mate were rescued by the coastguard. Within a few weeks, he was passing his nights on the sea again, but his wife told me that they were more determined now that their two young sons would not become fishermen.

The way of life of these country people lay naked to our urban eyes. In spite of new technologies, they had not changed much in hundreds of years; life was a struggle to survive and make small gains. The Saturday morning market brought in farmers with produce for sale who seemed to be unaware of which century they were living in. Flaubert had included a visit to Port en Bessin in *Bouvard et Pécuchet*. Seurat had painted many studies of the town, its harbour and cliffs, Simenon had set a novel here, *La Marie du port*; all of them had recorded a place outside history, anchored in its own isolated location in a cleft of the Normandy plateau.

But I had not crossed the Atlantic to live in a town that might have been a country town anywhere – in Ireland, for instance – for I felt I knew that kind of place already. I didn't want to know Port en Bessin, which no one had ever heard of, and so, as often as we could, we were elsewhere, driving off to more famous places: Honfleur, Rouen, Giverny, and farther afield, Mont Saint-Michel, Chartres, Paris, and the Loire valley. This was to be a feast of European places and culture, I thought, a chance of a lifetime for me and my children, and as the year progressed, regrets accumulated that there were so many places we would not see. We would not get to the Dordogne, or Brittany, or Burgundy, nor would we get to Spain or Belgium. I was replaying the role of Patrice who had, all those years before, introduced me to Europe and had rushed me around so that I would appreciate the true scale of the magnificence of France.

Towards the end, this madness of mine had accumulated other kinds of failures and regrets, and as I reluctantly allowed the pace to slacken, all those famous regions that were waiting for us were drained of their appeal. It was time to sit still, to opt out of history and geography, to find a place that was simply itself.

We had to leave the damp house on the quay because it had been rented to the summer visitors from Paris who took it every July. Monsieur Labbe felt he was evicting us and was pleased to find another place for us, the farmhouse a few miles inland, near Étréham, next to the stud farm where he had sent me to buy firewood at the beginning of the winter.

In the mornings there were swimming and sailing classes and other organized activities for schoolchildren in the town, and so, after I had driven the children, I returned to the farmyard for a quiet morning.

I had been a fan of Naipaul's work ever since picking up a Penguin edition of *In a Free State* in the early seventies. The story in that book, which goes inside the mind of an illiterate servant who accompanies his master from Bombay to Washington DC, struck a chord so that I became obsessed in a small way with Naipaul and his work, as if he and I had something in common. When I first read *The Enigma of Arrival*, it seemed to me that he was discovering a kind of solace in a place much like my own first landscape, the quiet place in Ireland that I had wanted to leave, and had left. But apart from these vague associations, I wasn't sure what it was that appealed to me in the book or why I should be sitting in this farmyard in Normandy rereading the words of that displaced Trinidadian of Hindu background.

★

Sitting on my beach chair one morning, I was distracted by a flock of swallows swerving upwards from behind the slated roofs. The vision was my madeleine, for suddenly I had slipped out of Naipaul's world and out of present time into that unnerving, mesmeric state of déjà vu. I felt certain I had seen these swallows before, and then as I came out of my brief trance, I knew: I was back in the enclosed cobblestone yard of my childhood. I was watching, more than thirty years before, a flock of swallows swoop over the roofs of the coach houses. It was the sudden swerve of the swallows, moving together in formation, which had hypnotized me.

"One swallow never made a summer," my father used to say, always his cautionary note a brake on the anticipation of bright things, but my memory was of swallows in summertime, like kites on a windy day diving and swooping through sunshine over the wide-open field that led down to the lake. Those swallows were my summers in childhood, yet they were also emblems of its end; a different picture – hundreds of them lined up on electric wires, now clearly migrants gathering in autumn for the departure for South Africa.

I was forty years old that year in Normandy, the mid-point of my life, if I were to follow my father's pattern and survive past eighty. I had settled in Montreal at the age of twenty-two, although I did not know that it was the beginning of settling; in fact, ever since childhood when I knew that I would be going away to boarding school, my life had been a process of unsettling, of not becoming too attached to any one place. It was my mother who wanted me to go away, to realize dreams of her own that had stayed with her, and so, cut off from my village home, I had believed that to bring dreams to fruition was more important than settling. I now know that I had not really settled in Montreal, although I had lived there for eighteen years.

I remembered those swallows darting and swerving in the damp air above the old yard of my childhood while the hens picked for stray grains between the stones. But now it was only a memory. My father was no longer there, nor my mother, nor my brother, for he had sold the farmhouse some years before. With the proceeds, he had built a state-of-the-art milking parlour and self-feeding system for his cows and a new house for himself and his wife. The house had not been abandoned in quite the way the Norman farmyard had been. It had been sold, and then sold a second time, as a country retreat for wealthy retired people who had earned their money abroad, in London and Saudi Arabia. The old cow house had become a swimming pool.

That year in Normandy had brought me back in ways I had not anticipated to the place I had left, had to leave – the first myth that had clothed my desire to become a European. But that desire had always been too anxious, and this long stay in

France had unexpectedly revived some inner bleeding of the scars of unsettling.

*

I know now that I was in mourning in Normandy as I read *The Enigma of Arrival*, as, I believe Naipaul is in mourning in that book. It is dedicated to his younger brother, Shiva, who died while V. S. was writing it, and ends with a return visit to Trinidad for the funeral of his younger sister. It is more the style of the writing than the description of the Hindu funeral rituals in Port of Spain that suggests to me that it is a book of loss. It is the personality of the man past middle age who has reached an end of some kind of weariness, more obvious now because it is the climate in which he uncovers a new landscape, the English landscape near Salisbury, as if seeing it for the first time.

What was it I had to mourn? My father had died some years before, long enough ago that I had almost forgotten the troubling dream I had had of walking without an umbrella and my sudden lapse into tears one evening at the supper-table, for no apparent reason at all, simply that I had suddenly felt overwhelmed by sadness. This was some months after his death; and then when I thought I had forgotten him, he kept coming back. The truth is that I was never very attached to him, never formed an adult bond with him; he was almost fifty when I was born; he was not an educated man, and we had no interests in common, yet I kept discovering ways in which I was truly his son.

If I was in mourning, it was not for my loss of him but for what I thought of as his own failure to live with self-possession; but this is fanciful, for even if he did at times seem to feel that he had lived at the mercy of others, I am sure there was much of his life that he enjoyed in his own way: fishing on the lake, shooting snipe, pheasants, and wild ducks, and card-playing with his neighbours on winter nights. And he had not suffered from any serious illness. He had lived out his whole life on the farm where he was born, although at the end, after my brother had sold the house, he seemed bewildered by the move to a new house that my mother had wished for.

My mourning had less to do with him or with any other person than it had to do with myself. Perhaps I was in mourning for the loss of that childhood home that my brother had sold or for that childhood landscape that was no longer mine. Perhaps I was in mourning for an Ireland that I had left behind almost twenty years earlier, not that I could identify any specific person or experience that I missed and deeply regretted, although I had a general sense, in making contact now with old friends and revisiting old places, that this was something that I must continue to do. During this year in Normandy, when it was easy to take the ferry to Ireland, we had visited three times, and each time I told myself that there was more pleasure than duty or anxiety in the visit, that my real life was rooted there still. Yet there was a weight of sadness that hung over these efforts to continue, as if I had in fact abandoned the place, torn myself wilfully away, and had made it impossible to renew the bond.

Perhaps Naipaul kept alive in me that general sense of abandonment and loss, an atmosphere compounded of vague regret, of irreparable separation, of time passing and leaving in its wake unfinished business, incomplete stories. It was a sense that that is how life is, that those who once experience displacement are forever hoping for a clean new beginning that will tidy up the past, close the book, or, if not, leave it open so that there are no regrets. The urbane Naipaul, who had gone to Oxford on scholarship and become a successful, London-based writer, a man from a colony who had become a master of English letters, revealed in *The Enigma of Arrival* a deep regret, a craving for something more rooted, more permanent, for an attachment that would fill an emptiness. And for the purposes of this book that attachment was to the seasonal rhythms of this countryside in Wiltshire that he had accidentally settled in.

It may be then that this disintegrating farmhouse – its layout so like the eighteenth-century farmhouse of my childhood – reminded me that the place and the people I had known and had assumed would continue forever through my lifetime, were gone. Yet the crumbling farmhouse was a comfort too in some way because it was mixed up with Naipaul's book, a record of displacements and erosions and new beginnings.

I found consolation in Naipaul's elegiac tone. He had found opportunity in displacement, a certainty that his experience had taught him to see more clearly, that his painful perceptions were the truth. He had spent decades fashioning reportage and fiction out of his travels in former colonies, in Africa, India, and the Americas, in former outposts of European culture that were now politically independent but in which people were still going through complex rituals of self-affirmation and evaluation, even as many Americans had continued to do in relation to Europe long after the United States was established. He had become fiercely single-minded, and those passages of bitterness or arrogance (condescending and even racist, some said) were part of a style that was refined and unmistakable. An impoverished outsider, he had journeyed to Europe and found his place as a great writer, and yet there were raw nerves that surfaced, a briskness that was complacent, a sadness that suffused certain writings, such as *The Enigma of Arrival*.

So did my sense of identification with the style of this book owe something to my own relationship to Europe, whatever that was now? I had gone to Normandy that year, and had dragged my wife and children along for an adventure that was surely connected to my own desire to be European, although, of course, being Irish by birth, I *was* European. I had grown up in a former colony of the British Empire and I was living in Canada in a former colony; Montreal was doubly a former colony, for Quebec was what remained of the former territories of New France. In my childhood and youth, I had felt a deep desire to be something other than I was: urban, cultured, properly European; and I had not managed to liberate myself from that desire.

I had made my wife and children hostages of my fantasy of being French, of being at ease in the middle-class milieu of European culture and power, of my inability to accept myself as I was. The years of unsettling had been long, and that year of failure had been long. I had set the standards too high for myself on this return journey, for my wife and children, since I wanted them to become European too, to be knowledgeable and appreciative in the way I imagined middle-class French people automatically were. But the year had taught me that that notion about France was a fantasy; I had trapped myself in old colonial attitudes, and I had made my family a victim of them too. I had given an imagined imperial authority, *la France* and its representatives, the right to judge me, and inevitably I had failed the test.

I now know Naipaul could not have helped me there, for if he was in mourning for the failures of a life, and overcoming that mourning by finding a style of elegiac celebration of his own migrations, what is palpable is that his yearning for attachment to place is a yearning for love. I do not recognize in myself any equivalent yearning for spiritual attachment to the earth, even though I have lost all faith in my childhood Catholicism. I may indeed have been in a state of spiritual loss, my mourning a recognition that travelling and cultural booty can never replace childhood faith, yet Naipaul's faith in writing as an enactment of knowledge and awe comes close.

The marriage I had jointly created in Montreal was the site of my deepest faith and then I had endangered it by imposing my burden on my wife and children. In attempting to go back and complete the desire that had been embedded in me as my father's child – to overcome the anxiety, the absence of self-possession – I had risked the bond I had forged in the new place, all this long after the desires and needs of childhood should have been surrendered.

*

It is more than twenty years since I sat in that farmyard in a state close to disintegration. The shame and anxiety that had gripped me in wholly irrational ways during that year would take time to overcome. I hadn't realized when we set off for Normandy that I would risk everything, that I too would sink.

What I had found was not *joie de vivre* but a sombre silence, as if history had weighed down the landscape and the people. *Le Risque-tout*, the name painted in blue on Pierre Labbe's *chalutier*, was a confident embrace of life on the open sea, of what had to be. He was a fisherman, as his ancestors had been, but soon, in my incessant interpretations of the scene, this shrewd Norman came to represent the ordinary people, the bystanders on this recurring battleground, minding their own business.

It took me some years to realize that "closed like an oyster" might describe me too, that whatever wars I had been through growing up in Ireland, or whatever wars my parents had been through, had sealed us inside ourselves. In that Irish farmyard, I had learned to build defensive fortifications. Ill at ease in the face of the outside world, in the face of its invitations and pleasures as well as its violations, the fortifications had taught me to strengthen my will and sharpen my suspicions behind a mask of silence. I might have been brought up to be Norman, to be shrewd and calculating, but instead I had become a dreamer, dreaming of escaping into another language, or of escaping into a language of my own.

I now recognize in myself some of those peasant Norman qualities of determination and survival, of trusting oneself to the open sea, of self-possession. I abandoned the effort of holding on to Ireland, the effort of pretending that all the places and friendships of my early life could be constantly renewed, that they still remained my deepest attachments. I abandoned the fantasy of being French, of judging myself by the degree to which I could think of myself as a cultured European.

In that farmhouse in Normandy, I began to accept myself as the father of North American children. They did not need to be colonized by my dreams and desires. And having accepted that fact, it became possible too to accept that childhood memories are of a time that has ended, of a place that is gone, and that their true place is in the language of elegy, rather than in the continuing daily round of living a marriage and raising children.

ELEVEN

Early in the morning, my friend Roberto and I drive from San José to Arajuela and then take the winding, narrow road through coffee plantations, up and up a thousand metres above the central valley into the cloud forest until we arrive at Volcan Poas. Roberto wanted to introduce me to the jungle, but today we have come to this volcano, for on previous visits he has failed to see it, so dense is the cloud cover at this altitude.

We must go on foot to reach the edge of the crater, on either side of our path canopies of *sombrilla del pobre*. I have read about the giant leaves of this plant, perhaps a metre across, but when I see it, I instantly recall the small forest of butterbur in the wild orchard of my childhood. In summers in that damp, green place, my brother and I used to walk between the apple trees, crouching beneath what we called "umbrellas," and then, a little older, we hacked our way through this jungle in search of a place to build our hideaway.

I try to shrug off the memory, thinking it is simply the accident of greenness, of excess of dampness, in this cloud forest. After all, it is the rainbow of orchids and tropical birds I have come to see. I have come from Montreal not for greenness but to purify my eyes with colours and my body with sounds and smells and unfamiliar juices: *tamarindo*, *cas*, *guanavana*. And perhaps if Roberto's desire is fulfilled, I will sense the untamed nature of the tropics and wonder at its inhuman power.

We walk on, greenness everywhere, and begin to regret that we have come in the rainy season. Will we indeed find the colours I have hoped for, that I have seen in splashes lower down, hibiscus in reds and yellows, bougainvillea, the pink "sausages" of the *chorizo*, and the passionate red of *malincha*, named after the lover of Hernan Cortes?

Suddenly I see yellow, a bush covered in small, pouch-like blooms. I look closer. Can this be the gorse that grew wild and spread out from the damp hollows, invading my father's fields? I look closer, at the vivid blooms and the hedgehog prickles that made the bush impossible to grasp. How can this be? What extraordinary feat of migration has taken place between this central valley of Costa Rica and my damp island in the North Atlantic?

I am walking again with my father to count the cattle in the far fields, and when he has checked that all is in order, he stops to do what I know he loves to do, set the gorse alight. As the flame takes hold, he cuts a small branch to use as a torch for spreading the fire to an adjoining bush. He cuts another branch for me, and soon with my flaming torch I am racing from bush to bush. When we have started little fires all around the clumps of gorse, we stand back to watch them grow into a great conflagration that sends sparks and lighting splinters in all directions. A thick cloud of smoke spirals upwards.

My father stands back from the heat and suffocating smoke that sometimes envelops us before sweeping upwards. He lights another cigarette as we wait for the great blaze to peak and then burn itself out. The supporting structure of these mounds of green and yellow is exposed and quickly burns to red and then black, the lighter branches falling off into the furnace, blackness spreading as the flames die down, all around the last tongues of flame licking the long grass.

It is a memory of more than fifty years ago, and my father died a decade after I left for Canada. I wonder why these ghostly visitations from a buried time are surfacing now? I try to shrug off such thoughts, to keep my attention on where I am, on this real place that I want to be free to experience as it is in itself. I want to be carried away by this untouched place.

The large farmhouse of many empty rooms and earlier prosperity was, as my mother said, a barracks, for she felt imprisoned in this place that should have been her home. I had read "The Kestrels," and these English stories of a club of friends filled my mind with ideas of adventure. I would go alone into the woods or out on the lake on my own adventures. Increasingly, my brother became interested in the farm work and the machinery, while I went off to reconnoitre an island for a possible clubhouse. As I grew older and began to read other kinds of books, my ideas changed on what an adventurous life might be. The flying adventures of Biggles took him far from England, and even better than *Robinson Crusoe* was *The Coral Island*. I read more and more, for it was through books that I was learning to travel and to want to travel further. The desert, the tropics, the jungle beckoned me away from the bald pastureland with fieldstone walls, the low grey skies and the damp, unleafed trees.

Now in the steaming jungle, I am confused by memory. This tropical place should hold its own secrets, should be known for itself in its own inhuman nature. What I had expected to be uniquely different, incomparable, is suddenly drawn into a net of associations buried inside me.

We walk on to the crater's edge. We can see only a few metres in front of the lookout fence. This lip of the precipice has a few scraggly growths, but, even here, it is evident that the landscape in front of us is one of rock, of molten substance from inside the earth. The fog is thick all over the crater, veils and veils so densely overlapping that the whiteness appears impenetrable. Yet, after a few minutes, off to the left, in the high valley, the veils begin to separate a little. What had seemed solid begins to dissolve into smoky wisps. In the distance, the fog thins out so that only a single veil drifts between us and a mountain slope.

Suddenly those drifting veils begin to move across over the crater, and we can catch glimpses of a sunlit rock face. The screen parts and closes and then parts again. It teases our desire to see the crater whole. We stand by the barrier gazing towards it. It is impossible to grasp its scale or its inner core.

And then the veils part long enough for us to have a sense of separate masses of cloud. One of these white cloud masses, thicker than the rest, seems to be spiralling upwards. Rock terraces inside the crater are revealed, some patterned in ancient black lava, some shadings of red and orange and brown, other eruptions weathered by the ages. The eye is carried to the centre of these terraces, and then it seems that the spiralling fumarole is like a tornado. What had seemed to be drifting cloud is now revealed to be an expanding column of dense steam driven with tremendous force from underground. It is billowing upwards from a luminous turquoise pool. There are smaller eruptions of steam from the edges of this viscous green lagoon, but the giant spiralling cloud is driven upwards into the heavens above this wide, wide crater. The intensity of its whiteness highlights the greenness of the still pool.

We gaze, mesmerized at these powers of nature so barely and temporarily restrained, until all too soon the veils drift over once more and the surface of this huge green well is lost to sight. We wait for this opening from the centre of the earth to become visible once more, and it does, a number of times, until the smell of sulphur escaping from the earth's bowels overwhelms us and our vigil must end.

We walk away along the trail into the dripping forest, soggy black earth underfoot, on either side giant ferns growing from tall stilts, searching for light and life. Underneath all, wet blackness and shadows, high overhead, luminous green.

I first saw ferns and grew to love them on the farm, and it was there too, I now remembered, that my mother had brought home from her shopping trip to Limerick the Classics Illustrated version of Jules Verne's *Journey to the Centre of the Earth*. She always kept me supplied with books, and even though there were large empty rooms in that home, they were no longer empty because I moved from one to the other, always reading, always finding a chair or a window seat where I could lose myself for hours. The windows on the upper storey looked out over large fields and woods, across the Shannon lake to the Tipperary hills, and often in summer there were sailing races, dozens of white sails drifting on the still water at the farther shore, sometimes among them one or two sails a deep red.

My mother knew I had to leave that place to achieve anything with my life. Seen from boarding school, the farm came to represent the spare and puritan culture of my parents and of the parish: the hard work, the humourlessness, the incessant duty to care for animals, the silence, and the punishments for transgressions of narrow moral codes. The solitary freedom of those years of adventurous reading was lost to me. I no longer cared about journeys to the centre of the earth; the goal of my life was to reach the city.

And so through education I made my way to the city, to Dublin and on to Montreal. But the child's adventures in imagination, the search for the centre of the earth, continued in its own ways. Where now is the centre I have arrived at? Sometimes it seems all the cities, the books, the memories, the people, the events grow on me like new skins, as if, indeed, they might somehow be peeled back to reveal a centre, the essential self unveiled. At other times it seems that each year, with all its unanticipated discoveries, pleasures, births, and deaths, displaces what came before, a new self constantly emerging to respond to the needs of the new day. And then, when I look back, I know that so much of everything is forgotten and buried that the notion of recovered histories seems entirely fictional, and only the effort to seize the progress of each day offers any kind of centre at all.

*

On the way down the mountain from Poas, we stop at Chubascos. Roberto has known this place from earlier visits, and he wants to share its many pleasures with me. Once a *soda* with *refrescos* and snacks set back from the roadside under tall old trees, it has become an outdoor restaurant. The owners' extravagant love of colour led them to surround the dining area with flowerbeds, multicoloured impatiens everywhere, lush and radiant.

We sit on a large tiled terrace with a canopy and hanging baskets of flowers, each table draped in different solid colour. A lawn slopes to the edge of the ravine; deep below the tangled forest an invisible river can be heard cascading down. A serrated philodendron that I tried to cultivate in a pot in Montreal here rises to a height of twenty or thirty feet on the edge of the lawn. We celebrate our good fortune to be in such a place, a jungle that is also a garden.

Roberto orders a bottle of cabernet sauvignon from the Chilean vineyard Casillero del Diablo, and while we wait for it, he tells me the story of the vineyard, how during the revolution from Spanish rule, when many vineyards were plundered and destroyed, the owner had hidden his wine bottles in a mountain cave for twenty years. Years ago, Roberto had visited that vineyard with his father, a bon vivant landowner who spent days tasting wine throughout the countryside, who loved nothing better than to linger in the sunny outdoors, smoking cigars and telling stories to entertain his hosts.

Roberto is his son, for as we begin to drink, now as always, he tells stories of his childhood in Chile, each incident with his father a wondrous tale of grand gestures in a feudal world, his father, dead for many years, now the hero on horseback. In memory of his father, he orders steak, and I order *casado*, the traditional Costa Rican dish of rice, beans, and a variety of salads, cooked plantains, cheese, shredded meat, and tortillas. We celebrate again and again our good fortune to be here in this place and in each other's company. Life doesn't offer many such interludes. We can sit for hours on this terrace. Next to us is the Queen of the Night, its blooms hanging closed, but as Roberto tells me of its incomparable scent, he almost has me believing that night will fall soon so that its blooms can reopen.

I think of my mother's garden along one side of the long house, looking out across the fields and woods to the lake. It was she who told me the names of the flowers in her garden and when we went walking beyond the farm, she instructed me in identifying the different trees and plants in the hedgerows. I think of her desire to travel far away, to escape from her fate, or for me to travel to Tierra del Fuego or some other place that stood out in the atlas we studied together.

Two middle-aged men, Roberto and I have become children in this jungle, fear and pleasure balancing on the rim of our cloud-enveloped craters. This hot afternoon, Roberto feels at home here, in a paradise that he lost. He fled Chile after the coup against Allende. For years he could not return to visit his mother or his sister. His aging mother came to Montreal to visit him. His years in exile turned into years of settling, but it was years more before he realized and admitted to himself what was in fact happening. And although I was not an exile as he was, I too had followed that same path, day by day uprooting and settling in a new place and a new time.

We linger long on the terrace, looking out at the garden in the jungle, sifting the gains and the losses. We had become friends in our city of immigrants, of travellers carrying memories from every corner of the atlas, memories of war, of death and repression, of music, gardens, and childhood games. We had become travellers for whom everything left behind was a metaphor.

★

Everything is a metaphor for Roberto and not only because of his displacement from Chile; a sudden and major loss of sight had eroded his place in the world, and he had to find a new place to be. Our visit to the volcano was much more than a tourist expedition for him, or a reward for me, because I had actually come with him to be his companion and his occasional driver on a business trip. We had taken a day off to look into an abyss of dreams and memories; perhaps this would be his last glimpse of the jungle or of anything in nature.

In the years since the rare genetic condition, which is robbing him of his sight, began its irreversible work when he was in his early forties, he has become almost totally blind in one eye and substantially so in the other. The bleeding of the retina that could be cauterized with laser surgery at the price of blindness was part of a larger condition governing all his sensitive body tissue, the retina being the most sensitive organ and so the first to hemorrhage. Nobody could predict the progress of the disease or the ultimate devastation it would inflict.

Roberto had been a reader and a writer and an avid moviegoer, and in these years, as he was reduced to talk and occasional outings to the cinema, he had almost miraculously discovered a whole new life. His wife, who had worked in an import-export company, set up a small brokerage, selling basic foods – onions, potatoes, beans – to Central American countries. She buys from Canadian producers to fill the orders she and Roberto have won from small importers in Costa Rica, Nicaragua, Honduras, and El Salvador. He makes frequent trips to the region to meet these importers, to entertain them, to win their trust and loyalty and maintain it, to make sure that they pay on time, and all this he discovered he had the talent for as he became the ex-Chilean "Don Roberto."

His background as the son of a landowning father in Chile suddenly became an asset in trading with these men. He had watched his father do it years before, and it was work his super-efficient wife would have been unable to do—establish rapport in this macho world. His storytelling, his love of alcohol and cigars, his sense of performance, his patience and curiosity for uncovering the story in other people's lives, his sense of irony and his hearty laughs at his own jokes, his wit and charm all contributed to the invention of "Don Roberto," the Montreal businessman who speaks on the phone from his successful base in North America and who truly grows into this role on his visits south.

These visits balance the anxiety and pleasure for him; in visualizing and dramatizing the scripts of these encounters, his novelist's imagination restores to him an adventurous life, as adventurous as what he had earlier in reading and in the cinema. He now tells stories of meeting wild men who have learned about violence and the laws of survival from the snakes and the iguanas, of how his own life has been in danger in the lawless territories of Central America. But in these years his will to adapt to the unknown has been pitted against the wild and unpredictable forces inside his own body. The great play of his life is not the one he had anticipated in the first decades of exile when his dreams were political, of rescuing Chile from Pinochet's military dictatorship; now the great play is with the unknown futures of nature and time, and the discovery of courage.

Roberto had been a great admirer of Gabriel García Márquez, and the Central America he has discovered is not far removed from the world of *One Hundred Years of Solitude*. Our pleasure outing to the cloud forest and the volcano and then to the restaurant among the flowers is an attempt to catch the drama of nature itself, its sublime extremes a source of awe and pleasure, but in fact it is not really divorced from the daily life down below in the valleys.

The traders who live by their wits, who had to be shrewd to survive, also live extreme existential dramas in which life and death, reality and illusion are constantly in play. Many of them had lived through the fierce terror and slaughter of civil wars that had made human bodies merely small change in the marketplace of power. With their pick-up trucks and their confidence, they are creating new lives for themselves and their families, creating possibilities out of the ashes.

*

My father and mother were traders too, in a way – farmers who worked to produce food they could sell. They always lived in the farming community and had little sense of how the larger economy worked; they simply operated within the established ways of that countryside. My mother sold day-old chicks before she married and then full-grown turkeys at Christmastime. My father sold calves and lambs and pigs, in addition to the beef cattle he kept until they were three years old. I remember he went to the Saturday morning market in Limerick to sell apples from the orchard and onions from his large garden. I knew that his early morning departure for the city appealed to him for its suggestion of adventure and, perhaps, good luck; but this was not really his livelihood.

Their resource was the land on which everything grew and then the good luck with animals, with their fertility and good health, for it was a self-sustaining business: the cows that produced the milk every day, which was carried in tankards to the local creamery every morning, were also the cows that produced the calves that would eventually grow into bullocks and heifers that would be sold at the fair in Scariff. The cows grazed the fields, ate hay in winter that was harvested from the fields in summer, and root vegetables and oats that had been grown as crops, sown in spring, harvested in autumn. Much of the work on the farm sustained the cows for they were at the centre of the little economy, and it was all work in intimate contact with the earth, the ploughing, the planting, the harvesting.

I grew up helping with much of this work in season, although it never kept me away from school, for it had been decided that my brother would be the farmer and I would be sent out into the world. In winter I pulped the turnips and mangel-wurzels, the shredded vegetables falling bucketful by bucketful beneath the great wheel, my hands growing calluses as I swung the handle round and round. In spring I sat in the potato pit and cut the seed potatoes, making sure each piece had an "eye" for sprouting. In summer, on sheep-dipping day, I helped to round up the animals from far-flung fields and corralled them by the concrete tank in the iron-gate field, or rounded up the calves on castration day, and the cows for milking, evening after evening. Now after all the decades of travelling to cities, of working and living an urban life, I wonder what sense of nature I inherited from those childhood years, in what sense am I too a farmer?

My father was proud of how he used his fields, although he had no sentiment about how he was participating in the oldest and most essential of trades, the production and selling of food. He worked at a subsistence level and had no sense of accumulating wealth or profiting from market forces. He simply had animals and milk to sell as a result of his hard work. It was the way of life he inherited and he could not imagine any other. His closeness to nature was simply routine, work, and play, and it had no tremor for him of overarching significance.

He simply worked with what he had, "come rain, come shine," as he used to say. Nature was, most of all, for him, the weather. Much of his attention was devoted to observing the signs, trying to predict the next day, for the crops, the hay, the grass depended on the right balance of sun and rain. That knowledge was central to his life, although, typically for farmers who rarely rejoiced in anything, he complained when there was too much rain or too much heat. The weather showed its temperamental face constantly, and while the complaints were a staple of conversation, in fact, he was deeply stoical about it all. He knew what little control he had over anything and was skeptical of all human ambitions and hopes. The expression "saving the hay" seemed to reflect that wisdom, that all there was to hope for was the good weather that would allow him to snatch that small victory, what could be saved from the ungovernable flow of every day. In his quiet way, he had prepared me to appreciate the life of my friend Roberto.

*

I am no longer a country boy or the person I was when I left Ireland, or the person I was in the earlier decades of my life here in Montreal. I change in myself and am enveloped by change. Simply the scale of cities generates an energy for innovation, simply the friction of cultural differences a catalyst of changing attitudes and beliefs, yet there is a part of me that remains skeptical of the changes that cities generate. I am inclined not to share the confidence that politics, technology and commerce are infinitely progressive, that constant redefinitions and reinventions have more substance than fashion. The news is everywhere, the latest styles, the contemporary attitudes and expressions that float us through the days, and I too participate in these daily evolutions and transformations.

I do indeed live in this time and place, but when I travel in Central America with Roberto, I travel back in time to that place where my father spent his entire life and I my childhood, a way of life that I soon began to think of as nineteenth century in its forms and practices. My brother is the farmer now, and I could never be a farmer, or a trader in food, but there is something about my formation there close to the routines and the unpredictability of nature that is brought to life again, as if it has not been erased.

That part of Ireland had been touched by wars and revolutions, and radical change had taken place in the ownership and distribution of land two generations before I was born. The feudal age had finally ended. There were innovations in technology; electricity came to the farm when I was six, and tractors were beginning to displace horses, but I do have a vivid recollection of the fields being ploughed by our two horses, Bob and Charlie, and of circling the hayfields, turning each sward upwards to the sun for drying, in my hand a two-pronged fork. It seemed that the essential relationship of man and nature in my father's world had been this way forever, that some things remain the same for as long as can be imagined.

I am not only a child again in Central America, I am my father's son. When I look into a volcano or into a polluted lake, I feel my short human life is only partly mine, although when I visit the farm again in memory, I have the same feeling. I have an overwhelming sense of nature as destroyer and provider, source of awe and beauty, and yet in my urban world I have become a creature of language, a teacher and writer. In trying to save some unexpected wonder out of each day to put into words, it seems that I am turning the grass to the sun, picking the Bramleys and the Beauty of Bath for my father to bring to market, simply harvesting what has been provided.

TWELVE

Slievemore rises up to my left, as I stroll down to Dugort beach on the first morning in Achill. From the distance, it had seemed a picture-book mountain, standing alone, boggy ground sweeping up in a regular cone to a single peak. At its foot, it is more perpendicular, more of a hiker's challenge, yet still somewhat domesticated, the sheep grazing on its sides, the clouds gently descending and then rising on its upper reaches. I consider climbing it another day, but it does not invite me there and then, as mountains in the Adirondacks or the Rockies had, theirs an invitation to enter a decidedly separate kingdom of high plateaus and thin air.

I reach the strand and head westwards, past the rudimentary hotel, not much more than an extension of a pub. Sheltered by the mountain from the westerly winds, a few trees struggle to attain a modest height; blackthorns, gorse, and brambles make efforts to reach over stone walls but are bent over and down. The salt wind rules. I quickly realize that this side of the island is impassable, or at least I come to the end of the road, and as far as I can see, the rocky side of Slievemore, the side facing the sea, spills down to high rugged cliffs. I can imagine that farther on, toward the open sea, beyond this pastoral enclave, the rock and the ocean, the wind and the light must do battle. Soft, boggy interior; rock, ocean, impenetrable limits; has Seamus Heaney been here?

A day earlier I had driven away from the farm in Clare, through Galway and Mayo, and the spirit of Heaney drove with me, in my mind that poem of County Clare when the poet drives west to the Burren coast. It is a perfect Heaney poem and for me especially satisfying because it speaks of a place I know so well, my primal landscape. I can see that wild ocean off Liscannor, Doolin, or Ballyvaughan where "the wind and the light are working off each other," and I can see too my lake on the Shannon, or Yeats's tiny pond at Coole, or one of the many slate-grey lakes of this countryside with "the earthed lightning of a flock of swans." Suddenly, at the end of the poem, the illusion that this is simply another drive through windswept places is shattered by buffetings that "catch the heart off guard and blow it open." And there it ends, "Postscript," the last poem in *Opened Ground*. A closed book, a heart blown open, last words returning the reader to his own life in the world.

I remember the first time I read the poem in Montreal. I gasped with excitement and fear, carried off by the gust in the last line, perhaps remembering a wintry Canadian road when a storm caught my Volkswagen van and I momentarily lost control, or, more likely, carried off onto another level of being by the very notion of that open heart, the purity of it, the escape from all the conditions of aging to a renewal of feeling and perception, carried away and carried back.

"Postscript" puts into words the landscape I have known and seen, Yeats at the back of the poet's mind as he drives, just as Heaney himself is at the back of mine. Is it possible to drive anywhere in Ireland without such ghosts? I am in very familiar terrain.

I return to the sandy beach that curves gently for a few hundred yards to a jagged point. Waves unroll themselves slowly along its length, breaking first at the west end, spilling a milky foam that runs on and on forever along this almost level strand. I am the only person here, the sound of the breakers filling the whole space. Rainclouds, veils of rain, and mist thicken and then clear overhead and out to sea. Some miles across the water I can make out land, another island, perhaps, a peninsula, I cannot tell, for although I know this island reaches out into the ocean farther than any other, there are many headlands competing for this honour along the fragmented Atlantic coastline. A black dog brings me a piece of driftwood, and I toss it for him into the eddying shallows.

I walk to the farther end and up the steep slope to the road, over low sand dunes. A cluster of whitewashed cottages is arranged in a traditional pattern of Gaelic communities known as a *clochan*. There is a long view now and I can see the northern shore. I am close enough to see houses scattered along the peninsula. There are fishing boats on the sound.

The long, watercolour views are serene and sleepy in the half-light. I meet nobody on my walk. It is all still, easily framed in a picture postcard, a West of Ireland scene. My heart is not blown open.

*

On my first morning on Achill, I opened Thomas Hardy's *The Return of the Native*. I had brought the novel with me because I thought I would write something about my own homecoming. I imagined that I had grown up in a nineteenth-century ethos on that farm in Clare. I thought Hardy would take me back, not fifty but one hundred years to a small enclosed place untouched by modernity.

I had forgotten his ponderous mythologizing about Egdon Heath, the small patch of moorland near his home in Dorset that became in his imagination a place where civilization and nature fought epic battles. He wondered if Lear, the ancient king of Wessex, had lived there. But it is not Shakespearean versions of history that attract him; it is the landscape itself, its geological and "natural" condition: "everything around and underneath had been from prehistoric times as unaltered as the stars overhead." Even the sea, he claims, cannot offer such a symbol of "ancient permanence." This unchanging nature comforted him, for it "gave ballast to the mind adrift on change, harassed by the irrepressible New."

This phrase "ballast to the mind" jumped out at me, not because I was drawn in by Hardy's great drama of the Ancient and the New, but for some other reason; the very notion in that phrase gave me a rush of adrenalin, the possibility that such "ballast" could be found. It may have connected with Heaney's poem of the "earthed lightning" and the open heart.

My house in Montreal is one of five built as a small terrace more than a hundred years ago. The façade of the terrace is constructed of large blocks of red sandstone. When we bought the house thirty years ago, I was told that this stone had originated in the Clyde in Scotland. Ships travelling to Canada for raw materials used the stone as ballast on the westbound journey. As the hold was emptied to make way for cargo, the stone was abandoned on the docks and an enterprising builder had made good use of it. This Victorian home in the centre of Montreal has ballast for my Canadian self, and not only in its stonework. It is where my heart gradually opened, my children grew up, my marriage became an anchor.

So why have I come here, tuned by Heaney's poem in my head? What do I expect to find on this Atlantic island?

Hardy's mythical "ballast" was marked by other convictions, adherence to something "unaltered," "ancient permanence," a touchstone of value in the face of the fashionable and the urbanized. In spite of my detachment from such nineteenth-century mythmaking, "ballast to the mind" did release me into a long stretch of writing about homecoming, and now I wonder why. Was it Hardy, or Achill, or my own state of mind that made this phrase echo for days as a kind of blessing on my work?

One day, as I drove from Dugort across the island and on out past Keel to Keem Bay, another poem by Heaney came back to me, a poem of a much earlier drive, around a peninsula, somewhere on this Atlantic coast. "The Peninsula" is about a time "When you have nothing more to say," in other words, a time of creative block, and while the drive does not exactly provide inspiration other than for this poem, it does say how that inspiration may be found: "you will uncode all landscapes / By this: things founded clean on their own shapes."

The central irony of Heaney is here: he was the farm boy who looked with a fresh eye and heard with a fresh ear, the boy who became educated in literary sensibilities, and in that light articulated his own original "ground." For the Northern Irish poet, everything was coded with the murderous sectarian and historical codes, yet the image of possibility, of what is free of culture, free of prior interpretation and literary influence, was inspiring: "things founded clean on their own shapes."

Rocks, mountains, foreshore are ballast for the soaring,

buffeted minds of artists like Hardy and Heaney who actually go to such places, the rugged shapes carved by elemental forces that are ahistorical, "Water and ground in their extremity," as Heaney put it. And he could still experience there that pristine geological state, that solidity and authenticity, as it were, before human histories and cultural coding began.

★

These Western places assumed cultural meanings in the work of Yeats and others to such a degree that for someone like me, displaced early from the farm in Clare, from this West of Ireland, the ballast may not be the rocks, the landscape itself, but the poems written about it, the memorializing of the place in that literature. Hardy's "ballast" was not, to me, the landscape itself but his belief in the power of the literary imagination to make a poetic description overawe the reader, as Shakespeare's presence in the landscape had overawed him, so that the reader too would be anchored by a belief in that power.

"The Peninsula" strips away all literary and cultural allusions in its simple account of a day's drive by the sea, and yet it seems to get to the essence of that myth of the Atlantic coast. In it Heaney seems to summon up, in his own easy way, a century of cultural mythologizing about the nature of the West of Ireland experience. From Yeats's childhood in Sligo and his visits to Lady Gregory at Coole Park as a young man, he had it in his bones, and in his spiritualisitic soul, and it was he who encouraged Synge to leave Paris and go to the Aran Islands. But earlier in the eighteen nineties, the journey westwards had become popular for the leaders of the Gaelic revival movement and their disciples, something that deeply affected the Joyce of "The Dead," for, of course, Gretta Conroy, as well as Nora Barnacle, came from the West.

Donegal, Connemara, and Kerry gained a primal significance in the revivalist cultural nationalism that dominated Irish life for almost a century, and in that myth of authenticity, Achill had a special place. It provided the visual imagery of that movement in the landscape paintings of Paul Henry and his heroic iconography of fishermen, for, somewhat like Synge, Henry left Paris and had a conversion experience on Achill in 1910; he stayed almost ten years, and his whole life as a painter from this time on is rooted in the images he found on this island. It is 2003; the largest ever retrospective of Henry's work is about to open at the National Gallery of Ireland. "For generations of viewers, Paul Henry's work has been synonymous with notions of the essence of Ireland," the brochure says, "particularly the rural west of Ireland and a way of life that has almost vanished." The only equivocation here is in "notions of" and that is a hint of recent revisionism. Paul Henry may not have been promoted as the official painter of the spirit of the independent nation, but his critical and commercial success gave him and his style that status.

For a hundred years, city and town dwellers have made pilgrimages to places like Aran and Achill, and parts of the West have now become oversettled with chalets and commodified by the tourist business. As natural wonders, they are not always as awe-inspiring as the Canadian Rockies, for instance, or the Alps, or the Pacific off Vancouver Island, yet for many people these are beautiful, wild places where the heart can be blown open.

I did not grow up on this island, or on any of the celebrated

Gaelic-speaking islands along the ocean. The farm overlooked Lough Derg, not far from Yeats's tower and the lake at Coole Park. Montreal became home, and thirty years went by, during which time I often returned to Ireland. This was not really a homecoming in any dramatic sense. When I decided to stay in Achill in the middle of winter, I had simply wanted a landscape with sea, a wild and quiet place to write, but for years homecoming had presented itself insistently as an experience that must be written about.

★

I realized that I had left Ireland partly because I could not feel that kind of attachment to the place, the country, the nation that the great mythologizers had made mandatory in their revivalist project. That project was simple, in their vision of it: to "de-anglicize" Ireland. It was to become a political and military project eventually, but during the period of promoting Home Rule, the political agenda was often advanced by other means. Although I had learned the Irish language, and had felt a real fervour for a period in boarding school, during my later adolescence the Gaelic League project, the de-anglicization of Ireland, had failed to hold my fervour.

It did not provide the ballast I needed; by the sixties, that post-colonial chauvinism carried little weight. There was the Vietnam War to think about, apartheid in South Africa, homeless people in Dublin; there was another kind of politics that engaged me. And so notions of the essential spirit of Ireland felt claustrophobic to me. After all, I had become a student of literature. I was reading Shakespeare, Emily Dickinson, Henry

James, and T.S. Eliot; what did any of this have to do with Ireland? Yeats and Joyce wrote of Ireland, but the reason they were great writers was not that. They were respected and honoured for their internationalism; their art was nourished by literatures and philosophies of many cultures and epochs.

If the nationalist mythologizers found in the West of Ireland a symbol of a pre-colonial condition that they aspired to revive, an idea of Ireland that was elemental and authentic, the writers found there material that would free them from the pressures of artistic trends and fashions of the metropolitan centres; they were freed from the contemporary and the commercial. They found a way of life there that could easily be imagined in classic forms, in Greek tragedy, in Homeric and Celtic epic, in ballads and love songs.

Seamus Heaney extended into another generation that same impulse to find in the local place the images and the style that would carry him beyond Ireland and into a world culture. He lived in a time of deconstruction and demythologizing, yet it was not these cleansing operations that offered him conviction. It was the words of Yeats and Wordsworth and Milosz and Dante in his head.

He tried to believe that the wind and the light of the Atlantic opened his heart to a knowledge of things that are simply themselves. Travelling the Atlantic coast, he turned over another page of the country book he has been reading and re-reading since the earliest poems of Mossbawn and Anahorish: "bedding the locale / in the utterance." He found many ways to read the farms and lakes and their topography, yet there was a conviction in the return of the farm boy that he had found there a ballast that was forever his.

Who can separate the ballast from the fine-tuned eloquence that articulates it? Are the lines of Heaney that are most memorable, classic, a reflection of his superior powers of observation, of his deep attachment to his earliest place, or of his ability to breathe in the words of classic literary utterances so that they are faint echoes in his own utterances? When Seamus Heaney's heart was blown open on the coast of Clare, is it possible that what he felt is elemental, free of all mythologies, or is the wind from the Atlantic freighted with voices that have also been free to articulate clean forms?

*

Although I am at home in my house in Montreal and in the city, and I have awe-inspiring landscapes within driving distance, the Adirondacks and the Atlantic coast in Maine, I have discovered that the ballast my imagination needs is in the literature of a local place. Like Hardy and Wessex, I am drawn back to an Ireland of the mind, believing, in spite of the new thoughts that have occupied me in my decades in North America, that there is something permanent to which I can turn, a place to begin.

One morning as I sat at my desk, looking out at the sheep grazing on the brown slope of Krinnuck, a retired Achill schoolteacher knocked on my window. This local historian wanted to show me the real Achill. I was to be his guest for a morning so he could drive me to all those places that made the island special to him.

He pointed out prehistoric markers across fields grown wild with yellowing gorse, speculated about the reasons why a stone village of the nineteenth century was abandoned, showed me the exact Atlantic headland where Paul Henry's "conversion" took place in 1910, and the house of Captain Boycott in which the American painter Robert Henri had lived for a decade of summers in the twenties. He took me to the Mission Settlement where a Protestant community was established at the time of the Famine, and to Keem Bay to tell me about the Basking Shark Fisheries; he had worked summers there in the canteen when he was a schoolboy and recalled the tragedy of the photographers who were swept into the ocean as they filmed the netting of the sharks. He told me of the declining population on Achill over the decades of his lifetime, of the disappearance of the Irish language there, and of his efforts to find work for the community that now survived precariously on tourist earnings. There were clusters of new cottages and bungalows everywhere, all unoccupied for most of the year. These locked-up cottages didn't help the people; they were profitable investments for urban dwellers. Here a potter had tried to make a go of it, here a French painter; there a woman from Dublin had retired.

Every stone and bay had a story, every hill and lake a history, every turn of the road merited a commentary. The delight that animated him was the conviction that the spirit of this place was unique. Even in its decline and transformations, Achill made him proud. He was anchored in his place, and the stream of words that came from this old man was a tribute of love.

As we passed through Dooagh village, he pointed out the cottage that John McGahern had lived in thirty years before when he was writing *The Leavetaking*. He and the novelist often sat for a pint in the nearby pub. McGahern was never on the farm of my birth in Clare, but he knew it like the palm of his hand. More than anyone, McGahern offered me ballast for my years in Canada, ballast to the mind as I learned how to read him and then through his eyes how to read so much of European literature. He, more than my years of university studies, taught me how to read and after that how to write. He, more than any other mentor, or favourite author, has taught me what ballast is and how necessary it is.

Reading *The Dark*, and rereading it, my heart was blown open, but it was a pained and painful wonder that I felt. The novel and a volume of stories of the late sixties, *Nightlines*, are the most eloquent evidence I know for why leaving that Ireland was necessary for psychic survival, for me as for McGahern. After some years, the author quietly returned, to Achill, where he wrote his next novel, an account of a young teacher who must leave Ireland because he has married in a registry office in London. That return to the landscape of the west of Ireland, and then to the place of his childhood in Leitrim, renewed his writing in ways that led on to his final novel, *That They May Face the Rising Sun*. It renders immortal the place he lived in for more than thirty years, a quiet place by a lake where little happens and yet the essential events of a life are present and are placed in a luminous landscape. This novel is the culmination of the art he practised for decades. It has the stillness of a Vermeer or a Rembrandt. His American publisher renamed it *By the Lake*, but the original title captures his intention: *That They May Face the Rising Sun*. As all things pass away, he seems to say, this record of this time and place remains, this dream of permanence, this ballast.

THIRTEEN

When my father died, we were "home for the summer," my two boys looking forward to weeks of adventures in the woods and around the lake, their sister only one year old and on her first visit. I did not know that he was in the hospital when we flew into Shannon Airport and I drove our rented car out to the farm; my mother had not wanted to upset me because she knew that we had made our holiday plans, and she did not realize that his stay in the hospital would be terminal.

He had lived on that farm for eighty years, had attended parish funerals during all those decades, and now as I stood next to my mother in the church, it was as if the whole parish walked by us. Many were too shy to say more than a mumbled "Sorry for your troubles." Large farmer hands firmly grasped my soft city hand. I was a stranger, someone who had left early and gone far away, but I was included in the ritual; this was their communal means of accepting death as a fact of life – loss and awe and each other's transience.

I was a child again in that church, the parish assembled for this event as it did for Sunday Mass celebrated in Latin, a child attending an adult ritual, hushed again by the solemnity and deference of those heavily dressed country people. As individuals came toward me, I recognized faces in the crowd that I was a part of each Sunday decades earlier, then a generation older than me and now in their old age, and with people of my own generation who bore the faces that had been frozen in my memory in their school-time versions. Those childish bodies were now adult, and in all the years I had spent away, I too had become an adult.

I was my mother's support, and next to me were my wife and children. It was impossible that I should feel myself the child I had been at Sunday Masses years before, yet my inclusion in this religious and communal ritual eroded the years between, the years of growing into urban and educated ways of thinking. For a brief time, the sadness and the awe, the finality of one life, and of all life, dissolved my adult self.

Being with those country people, listening to that country priest, "dust thou art and into dust thou shalt return," brought back to me for a few minutes the sensation of unquestioned belief, such as I had known in this church. "Unless you become like one of these, my little ones, ye shall not enter the kingdom of heaven." I had heard it often when I was a little one, although I had not known that innocence had a moral or psychological meaning. My catechism had pictures of Jesus in his conventional beard and robe gently touching the heads of the children about him. Or when the words "feed my lambs, feed my sheep" were intoned in the gospel, those country metaphors made it easy for us to think of him as the Good Shepherd. My father was a good shepherd too, carrying back to the house sick lambs to warm them by the fire in the kitchen, but the words from the gospel were repeated so often that we all knew we were the dependent ones, the lambs and sheep.

That sense of powerlessness in the hands of time was the overarching truth: "For ye know not the day nor the hour." We ended each day by kneeling on the cold kitchen tiles to recite the five decades of the rosary, with its Joyful, Sorrowful, and Glorious Mysteries, my mother leading, followed by my father, my brother, and me, each of us taking our place in another communal ritual, acknowledging truths that were at once comforting and deeply disturbing to a young child who took the words seriously.

My father may have heard the words of helplessness and dependence, of the need to remain childlike throughout his lifetime, and taken them to heart. Many of the people who came to the funeral spoke of his gentleness. They remembered his smiling acceptance of everyone. He had not entered into conflict or conveyed a silent sense of disapproval, as many country people do. He did not confront or compete; in fact, he had always avoided engagement in social activities, as far as I knew, and this might be seen as benign self-effacement.

In some people's eyes, he remained an innocent, but I did not associate this quality with his religious belief. In fact, for a long time, I had assumed that he did not have any, that he simply participated in the communal rituals because my mother believed, and he could not give scandal to his children or to others by declaring himself to be a freethinker. Yet he was casual about Confession and Communion went only for the absolutely required Easter duties, and had made remarks about the only freethinker in the parish that led me to conclude that he secretly admired him. Other comments on priests, their comfortable lives, and the power they had to bully people, suggested that in his private thoughts he did not believe at all, or that his innocent belief had been destroyed. Yet he remained childlike in his gentleness, rather than becoming cynical or angry because of earlier disillusionments.

It seemed appropriate that his funeral included him in something larger than himself, although the religious ceremony was, perhaps, for him a veneer on a natural ritual of the place. He had his own kind of communion with the natural world. It all felt right as we moved from the church to Clonrush, to the open grave in the cemetery overlooking the lake. The woods and the lake were the site of his most intense joy during those times when he left frustrations and disappointments behind, and I had been there with him. The smoke of his Sweet Afton drifted upwards to the "deep blue" of the silent heavens, and the words of Robert Burns echoed in my head.

*

When I was a pupil in Lakyle National School, half a century ago, I was inspired to draw an historical map of our parish. I must have been about ten years old, and so impressed was a friend of the family from England that he had some antiqued copies made by a draughtsman he knew. I might well have forgotten about it altogether, but it came back to me in circumstances I could not ignore.

It was the day of my mother's funeral, almost thirty years after my father had died. Three days earlier, my niece phoned just after we had checked into a hotel in Ottawa for a wedding. We had taken the first plane we could get from Montreal and made it to her bedside in the cardiac unit in the hospital in Limerick a few hours before her deep sleep ended. My brother and his wife and daughters, who all lived a stone's throw from her house, took care of the funeral arrangements.

The undertaker came to my brother's house. I recognized him when he sat to the kitchen table, even though I hadn't seen him for a very long time. He had a large farm supply store a few miles away, and my brother had been a customer for decades. He was also an auctioneer, and he had a petrol station. He was known for miles around as a very successful businessman. As soon as we had agreed on the text of the death notice, he would place it in the daily newspapers and on local radio. He presented a choice of coffins. We discussed the flower arrangements a friend of my mother's would prepare, and then the schedule of events over the next two days. They would follow the usual plan: he would collect the corpse at the mortuary on Monday morning, embalm the body, and the hearse would arrive with the coffin at my brother's house at four in the afternoon for visitation to begin at five. The community would pass through my brother's sitting room where we would greet everyone. The coffin would be closed at eight, and we would set out for the church. The priest would receive it, there would be prayers, and it would remain there until after the funeral Mass the following morning at eleven.

Everything happened exactly according to plan. Hundreds of people came to my brother's house and to the church. For hours we stood, and the flow was constant, each person offering me sympathy, neighbours and cousins, and neighbours of cousins, people I had never met, and people I might have met years before and forgotten, or did not recognize, friends of my mother I had heard her mention, distant cousins, friends of my brother, business associates, relatives of my sister-in-law, work colleagues of my nieces, all the generations, some formal, some informally attired, some able to look me in the eye, some hurrying by, some stopping to articulate a moment of sincere sympathy, heartfelt words that went beyond the ritual sympathies. My wife and son stood next to me as my mother's life was honoured in this place she had come to when she married my father sixty-seven years earlier.

Next day, after the funeral Mass, we followed the hearse to the graveyard in Clonrush, and her coffin was lowered in the earth next to where my father had been placed, his name now carved on a small stone. As the prayers were said, and the gravediggers began to toss shovelfuls of earth onto the coffin, I looked out across the grey waters of the lake. I did not find myself slipping back into any childhood faiths. I was not moved by any aspect of the religious ritual. It came to me as a social event, and rather than feeling any metaphysical or transcendent sensations, I was moved by how the local people played their parts in support of the bereaved and of each other. I felt supported and found myself thinking again of the blessings of belonging, and of separation, and of how we come to know our place.

After the burial, we adjourned for lunch to The Half Barrel, a pub in the village that had a reputation for good food. It was the local of my brother and his daughters. I had never been in this pub, but as soon as I walked in from the street, I recognized something on the wall. It was the antique map of the parish I had prepared in school, now framed and placed in a central location.

*

The impulse for drawing the map probably came from my discovery of a set of ruined houses along a disused lane at the edge of the farm. And I was also aware of a ruin with "gardens" down the fields towards the lake. It struck me that once upon a time, there were many more people living all around here, other families, and now there was almost no one. Bríd Coffey, a close neighbour and friend of my father, born in 1900, possessed the parish memory. She knew who everybody was related to for generations back, and in my childhood, her tracing of relations was a favourite pastime. She could identify those families that had once lived in the houses along the lane, and on every other lane in the parish. With her memory, I compiled the map. It really represents her world.

Of course, it is not historically accurate. It represents a kind of mythical community of overlapping generations, a wish to gather up what had been lost. But then I remind myself that during our lifetime we can incorporate about five generations: those who came before us, our grandparents, and those who come after us, our grandchildren, and those in between, so that, with a little imagination, we can live not only in our own time but possess an inter-generational sense of connection to family and place. This is, I think, what is meant by roots. Bríd Coffey was rooted, her world no larger than this parish and parts of the adjoining ones; life was manageable, knowable, and predictable.

For those who stay in their parish, this tracing of relations, this placing of people, is the lifeblood of their communal experience. But for those who are destined to leave, as I was, and I knew it, mapmaking must have a different meaning.

Why would the child that I was take an interest in making a historical map of his locality? My map was an effort to recover a past time, both mythical and real, just like any memoirs or speculations I come up with now. Not content to live only in the present, I need to go deeper than personal memory to construct historical images.

What did that child of long ago intuitively know? Was my

map really a record of absence, of all those who no longer existed in the parish; through, perhaps, famine or emigration, or the less dramatic forces of mortality or marriage, those families had disappeared. What I first uncovered were the ruins of abandoned homes and then the realization that the generations of life in a particular place can come to an end. I believe that in some way I felt I did not belong and had an unknown future ahead, a displaced future. I wanted to create something to hold on to, something that had local boundaries and depth, something that, in some visionary way, would locate me in time and history. But parish and county gave way to another kind of world; I was displaced into education and learning, a world without parish or county boundaries.

I have lived in the centre of Montreal for thirty years, my children have grown up here in the city, and now there are grandchildren too. Time has thickened in this place. With marriages and births, the sets of relationships grow more and more interwoven into a new fabric of family life. Memories and stories, dreams and ambitions, advice and experience are all handed around and savoured, repeated and lived through again and again at birthdays and Thanksgiving dinners and at Christmastime. And friends and neighbours are woven in too. We have an extended family here, a kind of community, but it is not a traditional country parish, and it could not be mapped or known in the same way.

*

Making a map of my parish before I left for boarding school was a first creative gesture in a sequence that in my thirties led me to want to write a historical novel of that place.

Some years before, on a visit home from Canada the year after my father died, I decided to investigate a family story about a woman called Elizabeth Rourke. She was my paternal great-grandmother, the wife of my namesake who had left County Clare for Australia in the 1850s. The Otago gold rush in the South Island of New Zealand brought speculators and panhandlers of all sorts from Australia and elsewhere. Denis opened a men's clothing shop in Dunedin, and Elizabeth – obviously an Irish-Australian – married him there. My grandfather was born in Dunedin in 1867.

My father had once told me that Elizabeth travelled to Ireland with her son and ended up in Galway gaol. She had been sentenced to a week in gaol, he said, for breaking into our house. The circumstances were unusual: Denis, the second son, had left Clare because he knew the farm would automatically pass to his older brother when their father died. However, some time in the 1870s, the older brother died without children, and so, Denis, in New Zealand, selling socks and trousers to gold-diggers, became heir to the farm. The family travelled to Ireland, but before Denis had established title to it, he too died, and my grandfather – the next in line, an only child – was still under age. A younger brother of Denis claimed the use of the land until the minor became of age, and Elizabeth appears to have been denied access to the house. In a fit of desperation, it seems, she attempted to squat in the house. She was brought to court and sentenced to gaol, although, of course, by law, a few years later she would live in the house with her son, and eventually she did live and die there with her grandchildren, including my father.

I found the records of Galway gaol for these years. The entry for Elizabeth revealed that she had actually been sentenced to a full year's imprisonment, for contempt of court. I concluded that her personal need had entangled her in the "Land War" raging at this time between landlords and tenants. She had nothing to do with rents, evictions, and famine; she was simply an outsider to the parish who wanted to begin her future life in that place.

I became obsessed with the image of this woman from the other side of the world, waiting to belong, wanting to root herself after her life of displacements. And I wanted to situate her in some version of the course of Irish history, or the history of migrations.

★

The parish memories of Bríd Coffey and Elizabeth Rourke's story were both keys to the world in Clare I had left behind, a world that had largely disappeared before I was born. That was the world my father had been born into, or had inherited from the generation before, although his father, growing up in Dunedin, and his mother, growing up in Tipperary, were not from the parish. They had not inherited the Famine and its aftermath in that place, the deaths and departures, the true history of those ruined houses at the edge of the farm. The names on my map would have meant little to them. They were outsiders. And so was my mother who brought me up to go away, to become an outsider.

Map and novel – the reconstruction of Elizabeth's world that I set about writing – were both, I now know, efforts to give order and meaning to the torrent of history that flows through every life, to find a secure anchor in a historical myth. They join other efforts I have made to arrest that flow, to trace unmarked paths, to recover history from the great simplifying narratives presented in school and in public commemorations, to find the reality of even one person's life in time and place.

In attempting to imagine Elizabeth's life, I wondered about that family she had married into and whose name I bear. Who were they, and why did her brothers and sisters-in-law cause her to be sent to gaol? Was her husband, Denis, a black sheep who was sent away to Australia, or did he choose to go away? I wondered about the legal system of entailment, the passing on of property to the first son, and to his first son, down through the generations. Elizabeth had no place in such a system. I wondered about something that seemed to mirror that patrilineal system: the family tree. And that too, for a time, became an obsession.

All over again, it seemed, I was constructing something like a map, this time not of the parish but of a family line through many generations. I thought how ridiculous this is, searching for my roots like a third generation Irish-American, when I know perfectly well my family history for generations. Once antiquated considerations of pedigree are stripped away, what is a family tree anyway? A fiction embroidered from some facts: a myth of coherence, of orderly succession, of belonging.

The bare bones of births, deaths, and marriages are given coherence at such a price that it has little historical or genetic truth. It privileges the male line, giving a kind of emphasis to fathers and sons, excluding the families of mothers in each generation, and not only relationships of mothers and daughters but of mothers and sons.

Mothers have always been outsiders in a family tree, and in writing the story of Elizabeth Rourke, I realized I would really be writing the story of outsiders. That was her importance to me. I would be writing my own inner story and in some sense situating it in a written history, although, of course, that historical narrative, whatever it might turn out to be, would have to be invented.

*

To attempt to write a historical novel requires a major commitment of creative energies. There has to be a deep need for such a commitment. The same is true of writing a memoir. There has to be a need that is in search of a shape, which probably goes back to childhood and the discovery that words – in print – have a transcending meaning and power.

Perhaps the explanations – the self-justifications, – that are given form are in the end less important than the power of articulation itself. It is what renews a culture. To sing is to lay claim to music; to put something into words on a page is to lay claim to poetry. Writing a memoir lays claim to an individuality that, in its singular truth, corrects the simplicities of all communal histories.

Even the history of a parish or of a family line is a fictional invention that serves the need of the writer more than anyone else, the need of the writer to find his or her place in that flow of events and lives, some recorded, many not, some obscured for a time, or forever. Always there are the invisible people, the forgotten, the expelled, the non-players in the common drama. Academic historians in recent times have devoted great efforts to acts of recovery, of the experience of women, most of all, and of other submerged population groups unacknowledged in histories of political movements or of those with power in matters of war and peace, conquest and oppression.

Starting out with my little map, and through the years when I devoted time to researching Elizabeth Rourke's nineteenth-century circumstances or the family history of her husband, I was attempting to create a vision of coherence, to connect imaginatively what could not be so in fact. For my father, the distance from his small world in Clare to my world in Montreal was immeasurable. He never visited us here; such a journey was beyond the reach of his imagination, and I think he may have died still puzzled by my need to go away.

My mother did visit us on two occasions in the forty years of her lifetime that I was here in my new world. She might have come more often if we had not travelled back so frequently ourselves. Our arrivals became a routine she could rely on. A remarkable thing happened as she moved through her late eighties. She became an avid reader of travel books. In her armchair, looking down across the Shannon field to the lake, one of her great pleasures became her journeys out to the world with Dervla Murphy, to India and Africa, Siberia and Eastern Europe. She had taught me about maps at a young age, and we had traced the journeys of her cousins, one to New Brunswick, for she had become a war bride, and the other, a nun, had spent her lifetime in Nigeria. My mother was closely attached to both these women and all three corresponded.

She was my first writer. I grew up waiting for the post, for the air letters with the foreign stamps, and then very soon she would sit down at the kitchen table and write back. My own departure and settling in Montreal may have simply continued an established pattern for her, the story of her life contained in those letters that travelled between her kitchen table in Clare and the faraway places of her imagination and mine: Kano and Fredericton and Montreal.

FOURTEEN

For decades I kept occasional journals in which I tried to record some passing event of significance, to isolate and capture its texture and its essential importance. From student days, I had assumed that poetry, fiction, and drama were the only literary genres worth reading and worth studying, and that anyone who aspired to articulate a valuable and lasting truth of their experience must work in those genres. Memoir-writing, travel, autobiography were little more, I thought, than overheard notes, the private record made public, and only of interest because they cast light on the person whose main business was poetry or fiction. Naipaul's *Finding the Centre* and *The Enigma of Arrival* changed my thinking, and then I discovered Montaigne and began to read more and more memoirs, essays, and literary non-fiction.

In the late eighties, in France, I came across a book that inspired my first memoir sketch. The slim, elegant book is called *La Place*, written by Annie Ernaux, a woman from a small village in Normandy. I read it in French and thought for a time that I would like to translate it, but I didn't bring back a copy to Montreal, and in any case, it was more the idea of what the book achieves that grew in my mind. Ernaux's book captures in brief passages of description the poetry of her father's life. Raised in poverty and in his first years working as a manual labourer, he later had a café and grocery store on the village square. He spent his days serving coffees, pastis, beers, and baguette sandwiches.

An uneducated man, he was not opinionated or flamboyant in any way. He simply served his customers with grace, day after day, and earned a very modest income to provide for Ernaux and her siblings. It is a deeply moving portrait of an obscure and largely eventless life, written in very simple language.

Ernaux had to learn how to put aside her higher education to draw her portrait of her father. The simplicity of her evocative style is deeply moving because it is his language, or, at least, it comes close to his consciousness, to how he would think or speak if he ever came to represent his own life. *La Place* is his place, his café, his village, his entire world, and Ernaux keeps her outside perspective to a minimum. His life is presented without sentimentality or glamour; there is an evenness of tone that is appropriate to the man who was her father, and the daughter-writer has concealed entirely any judgment she might have of how his life has been spent. She manages, nonetheless, to clothe with dignity the struggle of an ordinary life out of poverty.

I knew, of course, that Ernaux had been studying with care the man from another small Norman village who had perfected such writing more than a century earlier, but looking back now, I think I may have connected the book unconsciously with McGahern's fiction and his debt to Flaubert. Even though it is true that I began to write seriously about McGahern in the aftermath of that time in France, something else happened.

I decided to move out of journal-keeping and worked on my first memoir sketch. It was an attempt to capture something of my father's life, to try to write of him in his own place, as Ernaux had done. And I recall working on a piece at the same time about playing with my young daughter each evening after school, hopping on rocks along the seashore beneath the cliffs, and then as I pushed her on the swings feeling that my life was actually in a similar state, swinging.

These sketches were little more than photographs or watercolours, an effort to capture quickly a time and place, and to envelop them in a feeling about the subject. Like many family photographs, they are lost, no doubt buried somewhere in a filing cabinet. I have no wish to see them again. But writing now, I recall that first brief period when this kind of impulse was sparked by *La Place* and I realize that even then, in the first decade after my father died, something about the significance of his silent life was working in my imagination, and that in some way I had not realized, his place was still my place.

★

I am sitting across the dinner table from the older of my two sons. We are gathered to celebrate his leaving. He is not simply "moving out" – a casual expression for that rite of passage – for he has done that a number of times already. He is leaving the city and the country. This is something he has already done too, six months as an exchange student in Bogotá, a summer taking courses in Paris. But this time his leaving is different. He has to leave Montreal to find a job as an architect, to start a career. Our mourning is not evident, for we have disguised this ending as a beginning, something to celebrate.

It is noisy around the table. We have been eating and drinking for two hours. For some years now, we have assembled weekly for a leisurely Sunday dinner, all five of us, and sometimes with assorted friends or companions. My son is energetic and witty, as is his sister. They like to perform, especially if they have invited friends. After a glass or two of wine, they set each other up. These are occasions for repartee, good-humoured teasing, stretches of explosive laughter between the salad and the cheese. We are disguising this ending in a ritual of our continuing.

Yet this natural unravelling of our family seems less a progression than a circling. He is leaving our home here in Canada to circle back to the place I left, to try to find his future there. But, of course, Dublin is no longer the place I left. The Anglo-Irish city of the sixties was still at anchor in the centuries reflected in its musty facades. Georgian and Victorian streets absorbed the dampness and reflected little sunlight. It had not hosted a world fair like Expo 67, with Buckminster Fuller's geodesic dome promising a future of light and air for Montreal. That was a future that failed to arrive, and by the time the Olympics came to the city in 1976, the monuments to glory began to suffer from hubris. But eventually Dublin did have a celebration, its millennium as a European city, which seemed to free it for a renewed future.

The Dublin of the sixties survives now only in my memory or in the memories of those I shared that time with; but of that I am not even sure any longer. I am not sure that our recollections of the sixties would now coincide. Nor will my son's departure and arrival in Dublin resemble mine. My unease there was marked by my awareness of being a country boy. The city was not home to me. I lived there for five years, but I lived there as an outsider – tense, expectant, waiting to be invited in. Dublin will not strike my son as a strange and unknown culture. The new city and the young people who crowd its streets and greatly outnumber their elders are of his generation. Their signs and symbols don't need to be translated.

My arrival in Dublin and my arrival in Montreal were marked by an estrangement he will not know. Loneliness, perhaps, he will know, but not the estrangement that I called "culture shock."

Culture shock. Alienation. Exile. My old-fashioned words slip out now, unintended, and my younger son laughs. He has already lived in Dublin for a period. He "took a year off" and spent six months working in Rathmines, sharing a flat around the corner from where I lived as a student almost thirty years earlier. The ease of his own arrival and departure will surely be shared by his brother.

"What is that, anyway, Dad? 'Culture shock'?"

"Well, I don't think he will go through what I went through coming to Montreal." I avoid the direct question.

"But Dad! It just takes a short time until you get to know your way around. One city is like any other city." He seems to have proven this to his satisfaction already.

"I think it took me the most of twenty-five years," I said in hope that the big numbers would have some shock value.

"C'mon, Dad! You get to know some people – maybe a few months."

"There were many times I thought I was over it." I have had a few glasses of wine at this stage, able to risk a whole truth. "Maybe I never got over it."

"What are you talking about? You've belonged here for so long already. You have a house and plenty of friends."

"But, *tu sais*, you live so much in this world, *t'es un gars de Montréal, de nous autres*, you forget where I've come from."

"I know all that, but still, why would it take more than six months?"

"Well, let's put it this way. In twenty-five years, I felt I lived through a century and a half. You can't really know what I mean by 'culture shock.' " The solemnity of my declaration is lost in the jokes from the other end of the table.

We move on to the dessert, our family version of the ludlab a Polish friend had lovingly prepared for an earlier celebration. For years now, the chocolate cake has been the centrepiece of such celebrations; all three children have learned to make it.

Later I recall my statement and my son's reply. Of course, he is right. In Canada, I became an adult. The person I am known as now is the person I have become, especially the person known to my children. Perhaps they do know me better than I know myself.

Had my old-fashioned words about culture shock affirmed with too much certainty something about my migration that might have been true but wasn't? For some obscure reason, I wanted it to be true when in fact it was not.

And yet the attachment of my children to Montreal is different from mine. It is their first home, and if they are at ease travelling and settling elsewhere, this is perhaps their inheritance from me. Second-generation immigrants, they do not have my burdens or my desires, my sense of place or loss or freedom. They have been born into a different world and sense of the world; they are more at home in this world and may not need to ask questions or wonder if they have found the answers.

*

"So he's gone already?" Brid enquires.

We are having dinner with our friends Karl and Brid in a Brazilian restaurant. It is a family-run place filled with peasant artifacts, dolls and masks and banners on ceiling and walls reflecting an amalgam of native and Spanish icons, typical of the many cheap, ethnic restaurants that crowd this area around Saint-Laurent and Saint-Denis.

"In the end he just bought a one-way ticket to London, and he'll make his way to Dublin after a few days." I keep the report of his leaving factual.

"Lucky guy! He's going to love it!"

Soon after her arrival in Montreal, Brídmet Karl, and they have raised three children together. Her life in Montreal has been immediate and committed; from the time she arrived from Ireland, she has been a joiner of groups — school committees, feminist groups, cultural organizations. And yet for these twenty-five years she has been dreaming of her own return to Ireland, even as she became more and more involved in her life in the city. She is always waiting for the opportune moment when she can execute her new plan for the return; she would go "in a flash," she says with utter conviction.

"So what was it in the end, no work?" Karl asks.

Karl grew up in Montreal. The city is home. He has left it for a year or two at a time to study and work in New York, Toronto, and Africa, but he always returned. In recent years he has built a cottage in the lake country north of Montreal on land given to him by his father. It is the place he went to every summer when he was young. His teenage memories are often of those summer months, playing in a band with his friends, beer parties, visiting other cottages in this small Estonian community by the lake. A keen gardener and tree-planter, he could easily retire to this quiet country place only an hour's drive from the city.

But Karl was not born in Montreal. In fact, his story was

much like that of Iztok, whom I had met earlier. As a baby, he and his parents and siblings abandoned everything in Estonia. They managed to get west of the Soviet zone in the months before the German occupation ended and the Russians moved in. His first years were spent in a Displaced Persons' camp in Germany, while his father, a Lutheran pastor, came to Canada and prepared for the arrival and settlement of Estonian refugees across the country. Karl grew up, one of the hundreds of thousands of refugees who had fled various war zones for a post-war limbo until they eventually found a place in Canada. They had no thought of going back, at least not until the Communist regimes were overthrown or the starvation years ended.

"He got fed up doing bit jobs," my wife explains. "Look how many different places he worked in the past year since he graduated, always temporary, a day or a week at a time. And he is prepared to work in French."

"That's Montreal today." Karl's political beliefs are forthright. "The city is going down the drain. It's over. It's the politics; nobody wants to invest, unemployment rises, and soon no one wants to stay."

"But they say it's like that all over," Brid joins in. "There will be no more permanent and pensionable jobs. Our kids will all have contract work."

"Well, almost everyone in his graduating class at McGill has left the city already. I think it's the demoralization gets to you, the feeling that you're not appreciated for what you've spent years learning," my wife adds.

"And why should they stay?" I ask. "It's the Independence movement that's destroying the city for French Quebecers as much as for the rest of us."

"Just a minute there now," Bríd interjects. "All they want is to be *maîtres chez nous*, wasn't that how it was in the beginning? And what's wrong with that? It's the need for a homeland. We Irish know that."

"Yes, but what about us?" Karl asks. "It isn't enough to be bilingual, to speak the language; you can never feel at home."

Karl still speaks Estonian to his siblings, but as a boy he had grown into his new home in Canada. As with many immigrants, his new language took on a crucial importance, and he went on to become a journalist and a professor of journalism. Communication became his business. He does not speak Estonian to his children.

"Not feel at home in another language?" I wonder aloud.

"But you know that the guys have had French girlfriends," my wife points out. "He's leaving behind a girl whose first language is French."

"Not feel really at home?" Karl lets the words echo. "Is it language, I wonder, or even accent?"

★

The recording of those conversations more than a decade ago initiated a long period of memoir-writing. Simply, it was a moment that prompted me to take stock, to look back, to try to put a shape on the decades of my life as a father.

But as I worked, the ground shifted. When does a life stop for long enough to allow one to write a history? My older son did indeed go away to Dublin, and after that to Washington DC, and New York City, and then after many years, he returned to settle in Montreal. His French-speaking girlfriend became his wife, and their girls are growing up bilingual, speaking French to one parent, English to the other. Karl and Bríd did not move away to Dublin. Their children have grown up, gone away, and returned. In this decade, so much has happened in our lives as families, so much that seems to be the substance of our development and change as we grow older; and at the same time, so much of our day to day living seems rich with the imprints of other times, of theme and variation, of déjà vu, of some essential or archetypal patterns. In our freedom to change, and in the lightest of our decisions, we seem to be less ironclad in ourselves than we imagine, and, perhaps, less than others imagine also.

Even as my adult children began to wean me of my old vocabulary and of the feelings associated with those heavy words, and to teach me how to live, happily, in their present, I found myself drawn more and more into trying to find literary form for my experience of a life in time.

Over the years as my interest in reading memoirs developed, I did not think of how my own life might be told as a story, but I knew that I could never tell stories or write a novel, so how could I find the narrative line of a memoir? I used to think that the big change in my life was my migration from Ireland to Canada and that in some way the story had to be shaped around an ending and a beginning, but even though place and distinctive cultures, uprooting and settling and change, seem to be the given concerns of the story, I am no longer sure that it can be shaped around them. This process seems to be less about the narrative of what happened than about the search for ways of telling it. And in the end it strikes me that that may be the most honest reflection of the story of migration.

FIFTEEN

Portally Cove. The small cottage we found for rent for the winter months is high up on the plateau above the cove. This is not the wildest stretch of the Atlantic coastline. It is County Waterford, around the corner from the Irish Sea. Our attention was often drawn towards that corner, Wexford, for just along the coast is Hook Head Lighthouse. The sweeping beam from Hook Head was an almost constant presence in our cottage during the long nights, and we often watched the progress of the ships in daylight or as moving lights on the surface of the sea until they faded out on the southern horizon.

On calmer days, we walked down the steep pathways and then up again to the edge of the plateau on the far side. After scrambling up around rocks and patches of low shrubby vegetation, we followed an eastwards path along the edge of the plateau for five kilometres until we came to the next inlet, the fishing harbour of Dunmore East. Even in winter, there is delicate beauty on the plateau, patches of dense ground cover that flowers in spite of driving rain and salt winds, perhaps because it is equally exposed to sunshine and heat. We enjoyed that high exposure on the fine days, and this became one of our favourite walks. Once in a while, we would meet a walker like ourselves, but most often there would be no one, for there are no houses or farmland up here on this barren stretch. When we dressed for the weather, there was so much to appreciate: the freshest of air, the constantly changing light over the long sea view, the waves breaking over promontories and vast shelves of layered rock. This was a perfect walk into the village where a coffee shop awaited us, or, on the slope above the harbour, the aging Haven Hotel and a glass of red wine before an open fire.

Our cottage had a spectacular location for the sea views, and that was why we rented it, but over the months, it began to feel like an inhospitable place. We had wanted so much to live by the sea, and it was a long-standing promise to ourselves that we would not be satisfied any longer with a week or two in summer, and now we had the sea every day. It was a long winter. Spectacular lighting effects on the sea, glimmerings and glitterings, morning and evening, slowly lost their initial enchantment; the romantic beam from the lighthouse inserting its way into our bedroom became routine, the ships out on the sea predictable, as were the storms and the rain and the tides. We were happy to return to Montreal.

This coastline is certainly beautiful in its bleak spareness, the eternal drama of geological or climate change imperceptible, and perhaps a kind of monastic peace could be found here, but I became restless. We were in a part of the country unknown to me before this winter, but still it was Ireland. I knew I was in Ireland from the moment I settled there. It was a different Ireland from the one I had left or even the one I visited regularly in summertime, but it was undoubtedly my Ireland. I knew this most certainly because I knew it was not Montreal and that it had instantly reduced the reality of my adopted home to the quality of a movie I had seen recently.

The months in Portally Cove was the longest period of time I had lived in Ireland since I left the country more than thirty years before. It was an experiment: to return and live there as if it were daily life, not simply a holiday, or visiting our families, or a visit to mark a wedding or a funeral. To a degree, daily life took on a normal shape, in keeping with our wishes, but the loss of Montreal disturbed me, the shock that the place where all the important connections of my adult life had been set down over decades could so suddenly be left behind. And in spite of naming a place as one's home, Ireland or Montreal, in Waterford the feeling began to grow that attachment and displacement were not the important realities.

*

When I returned to Montreal, the reverse happened, as it always did. Ireland receded almost instantly, faster than ever, it seemed to me, a matter of a day or two. Montreal was restored to me as my most real place, and its reality made any other place, even the cottage on Portally Cove in County Waterford, the cliff path we followed into Dunmore East, the beach at Woodstown, or all the places associated with friends and family, the evenings of eating and drinking over many months, all that receded into the other, cinema world. I knew I had returned home. Montreal reasserted itself, even after so long an absence in that other, primal reality.

I always find this sensation of exchangeable realities disturbing. I have lived in a few other places for extended periods, but these two realities of Ireland and Montreal collide dangerously when I travel back and forth. This sensation calls into question the nature of my attachments to both places, to one place or the other, and then the nature of attachment itself.

How can I feel so at home in one place as I go about my daily life there, exclusively so, it seems, only to find I can remove myself and feel absolutely at home in the other place within a short period of time?

I know there are many Irish immigrants in North America and elsewhere who maintain a proud sense of primary attachment to the homeland. And this is true of other nationalities also. These are true exiles: homesick, nostalgic, most comfortable with others who have come from that same homeland, and only really happy when they speak of their last visit home or the next. They dream of going back permanently at some time in the future. Where they are is always a secondary reality, never a competing one, never one that claims them with that sense of a complete reality I have felt in Montreal.

For many years, I was like these exiles. Those were the years when I did not buy a house: fearful, unable to attach myself to a setting that would be right for the person I thought I was or might become. Easier to imagine oneself going back, if only that were possible. Maybe it was after I bought my house that I slipped into this later state of dual attachment, of immigration, or maybe it was not the house itself but when it became dense with the presences of my wife and children and with our collective memories of our lives together. And soon after the months in Portally Cove, the next generation of our family life began, so that our house is now a place where grandchildren come to play, to sleep over, to hear the stories I once read to my children, to celebrate with us the milestones of our being here. The house and the city have become enveloped with our presences, our networks of associations and memories, and our sense of ourselves permeated by what the city has given to us, our anchors.

I tell myself I have embraced wholeheartedly this long life in Montreal, but why does it slip away from me when I return to Ireland? Why is the divide so exclusive, so disturbing that I try to keep my unease to myself, so — and I do not want to admit it — so shameful? And yet I now believe that the reason I became a migrant in the first place and made Montreal home, and am now glad to return to it, is in some way due to this shame, to a shame that is somehow associated with choice and commitment.

★

It may be that the opposite of attachment is not detachment but betrayal. Attachment to place brings with it the responsibilities of communal life, of citizenship, perhaps even the sharing of the assumptions of others who have been attached since birth, assumptions of loyalty to the community and culture of that place, or even to the nation that occupies the larger territory. One's attachment is not to place itself — unless one is a farmer or a property owner — but to culture, community, to the people who assume that you are one of them, devoted to their beliefs and committed to their defence. To want to leave is to express dissatisfaction, to find them and their way of life limited, inadequate, to challenge the mythic history they have articulated to explain their singular identity.

Do such feelings come from the sense of ethnic distinctness that I absorbed in my childhood and youth and then rejected? I left Ireland as a young man in a sixties frame of mind, to feel more free and without thinking too much about any of this. Only in going back does it appear to be a weight, which I must assume is my guilt. Perhaps it is not only nationalism I breathed in until it became a part of me; perhaps it is that Catholic saying attributed to Jesus Christ: "He who is not with me is against me." In my childhood, I fell victim to the defensive coercion of either/or, this Catholic doctrine of exclusivity – although of course it is not only a Catholic mentality – and so to leave the country, to leave the faith, is to live forever after with that weight of an indissoluble sense of betrayed identity.

When I settled in Montreal, I discovered that the ethnic nationalism of *les Québécois* seems to impose a similar weight of coercive loyalty and betrayal. The political transitions, from being a colonized, Catholic community in the British Empire to being a province in an independent Canada to being a part of a multicultural modern state, had produced resistances. The phrase *Notre maître, le passé* was often referred to in conservative and Catholic commentaries on Quebec nationalism in earlier decades, but by the sixties, a more discreet motto shifted the emphasis. *Je me souviens* was inscribed on Quebec automobile licence plates. In both cases, one is defined by remembering, remaining loyal to, a mythological past, one version apparently voluntary, the earlier coercive, with strong overtones of patriarchal domination. The original settlers from Normandy and Brittany, in the early seventeenth century, and their descendants, have been given retrospective status as *les Québécois de souche*, in some sense the founding fathers and preservers of a normative national spirit.

I have lived through two fierce referendum campaigns about this very issue of loyalty and betrayal. The political discourse was about Quebec sovereignty or Canadian federalism; on the street, the debate was about being *maîtres chez nous* or commitment to living with the rest of Canada, whereas onlookers in other provinces talked of the process as "breaking up Canada." The deck of cards flipped in different ways: the pride of being independent for one was destruction and loss for the other; and even though I knew that so many wars in history and around the world flared up around inescapable ethnic conflicts, living in Canada encouraged one to believe in accommodation, compromise, federation. The chanting of *Le Québec aux Québécois* sounded like a tribal mantra from an earlier time when *les anglais* were masters for centuries after the defeat of the French empire in North America. Now in the decades of mass migrations, it reflected not so much a vengeful anglophobia as a sense of the invasion of the wider territory that a multicultural city like Montreal represented.

All I could think of during these referenda was the defensive mindset of exclusivity, of ethnocentric history, of a notion of purity that bestowed a sense of a sacred trust. There are often just and clear reasons for such territorial or tribal defensiveness for it is frequently the inheritance of imperial invasions, of necessary self-assertion and self-protection. But in Ireland notions of exclusivity and belonging had festered again into savagery and bloodshed during my first decade in Canada. Michael Ignatieff, a Canadian of Russian and Scottish ancestry, reflected on the sense of "blood and belonging" that governed the strife in Northern Ireland as well as the larger-scale barbarism that enveloped the territories of the former Yugoslavia, and touched also on the situation in Quebec. He was a passionate supporter of the "rights revolution" as a way of thinking that might lead away from civil wars and genocides. But Ignatieff is not naïve; he understands how blood so often informs belonging.

I can no longer believe in such certainties of belonging, of rootedness, of naming who I am. Neither place itself nor communal pieties or myths of history hold me, although all are part of who I am. Anchorage is more intimate, more temporary, more provisional, more open to the reality of time and to the fact that we are essentially impermanent creatures.

*

We need to anchor ourselves, each one of us: even that is perhaps too mechanical and solid a metaphor for the notion I have in mind. I want a word that acknowledges the passage of time, the fragile early threads of connection toughening with familiarity and repetition, winding together with other threads over months and years until they are indeed strong enough to hold an anchor, until, perhaps, at a later stage, the bond begins to erode, at the mercy of time and inattention, and a moment might even come when old threads fray altogether, and only a fading memory is left of what had once been a vitally important relationship or book or piece of music. While some people anchor themselves in memories, the pleasure of vivid recollection so real that time past is no longer past, I am inclined to think that remembering is a form of dreaming and imagining which allows us to recreate ourselves in the here and now.

A lifetime of friendships, of sports teams, of singers and writers who become obsessions, of cities and houses, one thing connecting to another, one thing appreciated or remembered in relation to another, new people woven into this web of associations, the greater part forgotten until perhaps a thread is pulled out of the rope. A photograph from boarding school, 1962, a street-map of the centre of Berlin, circa 1966, a mer from an Armenian restaurant in Manhattan in 1972, a program for a concert by young Yo-Yo Ma: I am a collector of such things, a hoarder of prompts to memory, and the feel of such objects still triggers a sense of connection to myself, my history, and my places. We are attached – we attach ourselves – to the most ordinary things and often in the most bizarre of ways that make little sense to other people, and we are attached to the most unlikely people for the craziest of reasons.

My souvenirs and their associated memories matter to me, for they connect me to the jet stream of myself, that vanishing trace of having once crossed this sky. It was that meaning I had hoped to capture in the word attachment, not the simple nostalgia of it, or the self-satisfaction of proving that I was there, once, or here, or any place at all. I had hoped to understand how it was that my disorganized collection of souvenirs in this disorganized house, as well as my haphazard memories and friendships, were signposts to an essential and evolving part of me.

Most of all, the flesh and blood intimacies of marriage, of being a father, the endless acts of attention of family life have created my deepest attachments, and in this case the word I need is love, but even these intimate bonds have been formed in time and continue to change over time. And so I regret the loss of that temporal nuance in the word attachment, the sense that in the end it is not the location of my life that is vital, it is the way in which I have learned to accommodate change in Montreal and in Ireland, for as we change constantly in ourselves over a lifetime so does the nature of our attachments. I wanted it to have that fragile and mysterious depth, that sense of the accidental and the arbitrary that reassures us of our own unique and tenacious individual history.

EPILOGUE

Much has changed since the winter in Portally Cove, and for some years now my wife and I spend every winter in Ireland. There are many reasons why this has come about: a medical need to get away from the permanently freezing temperatures of Montreal during those months, aging parents and the wish to spend more time with them after so long away, renewed friendships, and an increasing realization that my "Ireland" is a state of mind that I have discovered and created, less a state of mind than a state of words.

It may be that it was during the months in County Waterford I learned what I should always have known, may have known but had not realized fully. It is not place or history or even my own past that is my true anchor; I am most myself and becoming more myself as I discover more and more possibilities for communication. For decades, I felt tongue-tied or failed to discover a voice, but it was the struggle to speak that made this the real site of attachment in my life. Talking to my adult children long-distance, exchanging emails with them, and seeing my grandchildren on Skype brings me into their daily lives, into the future they are creating, and as they do this in their young lives, I feel not an outsider, an observer, but someone who is being recreated. My most precious attachment to their present and their future has replaced the old divided realities of place with a new reality.

I can be in my house in Montreal or Ireland, they can be in Asia or Europe or America, as they were variously during those months I spent in Waterford; this kind of communication has created a new dimension, the possibility that their daily lives elsewhere can be immediately a part of mine. Time zones and continental geographies disappear in this instantaneous talk. Rather than the technology itself creating the new reality, it is my recognition of it, my acceptance, which is what began to happen in Waterford.

All these fleeting words are the substance of our relationships, but they are part of my more comprehensive belief that it is language that has anchored me, the "state of words" formed inextricably of my own utterances and the words of others that have become a vital part of me. While we all live in the enveloping discourses of conversations and commentaries, radio and television making us all sound more and more like each other, my "state of words" is written and literary. Ever since I met my first artist, the solitary Dane on Inishere, I have been drawn to artists like Emily Dickinson, whose "letter to the world" was the confident testament of a person who had to establish her own place in obscure circumstances. Her voice is as real to me as that of Montaigne or Coetzee, W. B. Yeats or V. S. Naipaul. I have been drawn to literary art as a world I belong in most comfortably, and it is a world that can include Montreal and Ireland and all the other places.

My Ireland is in Irish writing most of all, especially in the work of John McGahern, in my writing about his work, and in that sense of sharing it with other readers who are powerfully drawn to it. For some people his work is grounded in a rural and normative voice, and it is clear that this aspect of it helps many readers to anchor themselves in their known world. He appears to celebrate a place that can be called Leitrim, and place names are a guarantee that he is rooted in that world, but it is not this that makes it my Ireland. I discovered his work here in Montreal, and I first met him here some years later, and over the years his words became a part of me in a way I cannot really understand. His work does not attach me to Leitrim, or to Clare, or to County Kilkenny, where I now spend much of my time, in that sense of being grounded in a local culture, but it does attach me to the work of all those writers who inhabit the imaginative state that illuminates his words from the inside. It is something like this I carry with me as I travel back and forth, and the more fully I inhabit it myself, the more I no longer need to reflect on attachment.

AUTHOR'S NOTE

I have given a particular focus here to events in which my life intersected with others. Many family members, friends, and public figures are referred to, some under their own names. I write in the wonder of understanding and the discovery of themes and variations in so many lives; it is not my intention to limit or judge others through the passing role they are given in this written kaleidoscope. In fact, I wish to thank all of them for the many ways in which they have enriched my life.

Over many years, earlier versions of some episodes have appeared in print or been broadcast on radio. I thank the editors whose reception of various essays has been a vital form of encouragement: Chris Agee at *Irish Pages: A Journal of Contemporary Writing,* Brendan Barrington at *Dublin Review,* Michael Redhill at *Brick: A Literary Journal,* Cliodhna Ni Anluain, producer of *Sunday Miscellany* on RTE Radio 1, and editor of *Sunday Miscellany: A Selection from 2006-2008* and *Sunday Miscellany: A Selection from 2008-2011*, and John Dillon and Nathaniel Myers of *Breac: A Digital Journal of Irish Studies.* I acknowledge their permission to reprint passages from this earlier work. I also acknowledge the work of Eamon Grennan and of Tom Lozar from which I have borrowed, in Eamon's case with especial thanks since he supplied my title.

George O'Brien, master of memoir writing, has been a patient reader of drafts over many years, and without his long-term friendship and example, this work would never have happened. I would also like to thank Mark Abley and Terence Killeen for their constant support and encouragement. Jonathan Williams undertook to find a publisher of an earlier version many years ago, and even when I had lost confidence, he was determined to go on. His belief in my work and his meticulous attention to the sentences have been a great gift, and my thanks to him now for once again doing the rounds of publishers on my behalf.

Finally, I thank Linda Leith for her courage in taking on the manuscript and her courtesy throughout the production process. I am indebted to Linda's designer, Debbie Geltner, for a beautiful looking book, and my proofreader, Emily Kitagawa, has cleaned up many sentences and did some eagle-eyed fact checking; my thanks to both.